Gourmet's
Five Ingredients

Gourmet's Five Ingredients

MORE THAN **175** EASY RECIPES FOR EVERY DAY

FROM THE EDITORS OF GOURMET

Condé Nast Books   Random House

New York

Library of Congress
Cataloging-in-Publication Data

Gourmet's five ingredients: more than 175 easy recipes for every day / from the editors of Gourmet

p. cm.

Includes index

ISBN 0-375-50866-X (alk. paper)

1. Quick and easy cookery. 2. Menus. I. Title: Five Ingredients. II. Gourmet Books, Inc.

TX833.5 .G685 2002

641.5'55—dc21   2002068042

Random House website address: www.atrandom.com

Some of the recipes in this work were published previously in *Gourmet* magazine.

Printed in the United States of America on acid-free paper

98765432

First Edition

All informative text in this book was written by Diane Keitt, Linda M. Immediato, Jane Daniels Lear, Zanne Stewart, and Shelton Wiseman.

The text of this book was set in Condé Nast Times Roman by Bill SMITH STUDIO.
The four-color separations were done by American Color, Applied Graphic Technologies, and Quad/Graphics, Inc. The book was printed and bound at R. R. Donnelley and Sons. Stock is Sterling Ultra Web Gloss, Westvāco.

For Random House

Lisa Faith Phillips, Vice President/General Manager
Tom Downing, Direct Marketing Director
Deborah Williams, Operations Director
Lyn Barris, Direct Marketing Manager
Fianna Reznik, Direct Marketing Associate
Eric Levy, Inventory Assistant
Eric Killer, Direct Marketing Assistant
Richard B. Elman, Production Manager

For Gourmet Books

Diane Keitt, Director
Linda M. Immediato, Associate Editor

For Gourmet Magazine

Ruth Reichl, Editor-in-Chief
Diana LaGuardia, Art Director

Zanne Early Stewart, Executive Food Editor
Kemp Miles Minifie, Senior Food Editor
Alexis M. Touchet, Associate Food Editor
Lori Walther Powell, Food Editor/Stylist
Amy Mastrangelo, Food Editor
Katy Massam, Food Editor
Shelton Wiseman, Food Editor
Ruth Cousineau, Food Editor
Gina Marie Miraglia, Food Editor
Melissa Roberts-Matar, Food Editor
Ian McLean Knauer, Food Editor

Romulo A. Yanes, Photographer

Produced in association with Bill SMITH STUDIO

Bill Smith, Publisher
Anne B. Wright, Project Editor
Maureen O'Connor, Production Editor
Marilyn Flaig, Indexer

Jacket and book design by Audrey Razgaitis and Diana LaGuardia.

Front Jacket: Tomato, Goat Cheese, and Onion Tart (page 78). Back Jacket: Salt and Pepper Shrimp (page 15); Vanilla-Bean Ice Cream (page 148); Baked Macaroni and Cheese with Stewed Tomatoes (page 37); Cider-Braised Pork Shoulder with Caramelized Onions (page 99); Pasta with Asparagus-Lemon Sauce (page 46); Turkey Burgers with Boursin (page 60); Peach Sangría (page 29); Fresh Mango and Cucumber Soup (page 113). Frontispiece: Turkey Burgers with Boursin (page 60).

Recipe Tips

- **Measure liquids** in glass or clear plastic liquid-measuring cups and **dry ingredients** in nesting dry-measuring cups (usually made of metal or plastic) that can be leveled off with a knife.

- **Measure flour** by spooning (not scooping) it into a dry-measuring cup and leveling off with a knife without tapping or shaking cup.

- Do not **sift flour** unless specified in recipe. If sifted flour is called for, sift flour before measuring. (Many brands say "presifted" on the label; disregard this.)

- When we call for a **shallow baking pan**, we mean an old-fashioned jelly-roll or four-sided cookie pan.

- **Measure skillets** and **baking pans** across the top, not across the bottom.

- To prepare a **water bath** for baking, put your filled pan in a larger pan and add enough boiling-hot water to reach halfway up the side of the smaller pan.

- Use light-colored **metal pans** for baking unless otherwise specified. If using dark metal pans, including nonstick, your baked goods will likely brown more and the cooking times may be shorter.

- Wash and dry all **produce** before using.

- Before prepping fresh **herbs or greens**, remove the leaves or fronds from the stems—the exception is cilantro, which has tender stems.

- When **salting water** for cooking, use 1 tablespoon salt for every 4 quarts of water.

- Black **pepper** in recipes is always freshly ground.

- Wear protective gloves when handling **chiles**.

- Grate **cheeses** just before using.

- To **zest** citrus fruits, remove the colored part of the rind only (avoid the bitter white pith). For strips, use a vegetable peeler. For grated zest, we prefer using a rasplike Microplane zester, which results in fluffier zest, so pack to measure.

- **Toast spices** in a dry heavy skillet over moderate heat, stirring, until fragrant and a shade or two darker. **Toast nuts** in a shallow baking pan in a 350°F oven until golden, 5 to 10 minutes. **Toast seeds** either way.

- To **peel** a tomato or peach, first cut an X in the end opposite the stem and immerse in boiling water (10 seconds for a tomato or 15 seconds for a peach). Transfer it to ice water and then peel.

131

50

10

92

40

30

83

141

125

108

contents

16

Introduction

THE DIRTY LITTLE SECRET of cooking is that shopping is the hardest part.

I didn't quite understand that until *Gourmet*'s cooks set out to create a series of recipes meant just for ourselves. We wanted dishes we could cook after a hard day at the office, and it suddenly became clear that we had become very spoiled: In *Gourmet*'s kitchens, the ingredients we need are delivered every day.

When we leave, however, things are different. Like you, we have to stop at the store on the way home to pick up all the things we don't have on hand. And frankly, standing on line at the grocery is the last thing I want to do at the end of a difficult day at work. Faced with the endless line at the checkout counter, I've been known to abandon my cart, sneak out of the store, pick up the phone, and order in.

There is a better way . . . and you'll find it in this book. These recipes require so few ingredients that if I plan ahead I can easily do an entire week's worth of shopping in one quick trip to the store.

But easy isn't everything; there's no point in making something quickly if it doesn't taste good. That is why the ten very demanding food editors standing at our stoves insist that each of these recipes meets the same criteria as all the others: It must be superb. If a recipe doesn't work with just a few ingredients, we don't resort to trickery and we don't decide to use it anyway; we simply move on.

So when you find a recipe for vanilla-bean ice cream in this book, you needn't worry that this is a compromise solution; there isn't a better recipe anywhere. The same holds true for our tomato, onion, and goat cheese tart, our fresh mango and cucumber soup, and our pork chops with apples and cream.

The secret lies in what we call "power ingredients"—eight categories of foods that really pack a punch. Everyday items that you're likely to have in your pantry, each makes the most of its flavor opportunities. You'll find the list on the next page. You'll also find a seasonal chart of menu ideas on page 158, as well as an index that tells you which recipes can be made in 30 minutes or less, and which ones can serve as a meal-in-one.

We have cheated, but just a little. We don't count water, salt, or pepper among the five ingredients. On the other hand, when was the last time you went to the store to buy any of those?

Ruth Reichl,
Editor-in-Chief

fat
cream
oil
crème fraîche
coconut milk
cheese
butter

hot
black pepper
red pepper flakes
curry paste
ginger
mustard
horseradish
chiles

sour
vinegar
tomatoes
wine
limes
oranges
grapefruit
lemons

salt
olives
capers
teriyaki sauce
soy sauce
Asian fish sauce
anchovies
salt

Power Ingredients

WHEN USING only five ingredients, you have to make each one count. These powerhouses do the work of many; you'll find at least one in every recipe.

sweet
sugar
fruit
maple syrup
bittersweet chocolate
flaked coconut
jelly
honey

onion
leeks
onions
scallions
shallots
garlic

cured meats
pancetta
prosciutto
Spanish chorizo
bacon

herbs
basil
cilantro
chives
dill
parsley
rosemary
sage
tarragon
thyme

HORS D'OEUVRES

Anchovy Puffs **18**

Parmesan Garlic Sticks **19**

Pecan Blue Cheese Crackers **20**

Pistachio Twists **18**

Potatoes Topped with Smoked Salmon and Fennel **15**

Prosciutto and Gruyère Pinwheels **19**

Salt and Pepper Shrimp **15**

Tuna Empanaditas **16**

APPETIZERS

Boston Lettuce Salad with Honey Mustard and Herbs **25**

Daikon Ginger Salad **25**

Jalapeño Cheddar Toasts **21**

Potato Latkes **23**

Quiche Lorraine **20**

Roasted Pepper Salad **24**

Slow-Roasted Tomatoes **21**

Two-Bean Salad **24**

Starters

many of the recipes in this section moonlight as both appetizer and hors d'oeuvre. Our tuna *empanaditas* make perfect cocktail companions or, served before our pork tenderloin with *mojo*, equally tantalizing appetizers. Slow-roasted tomatoes on toasted baguette slices—a variation on bruschetta— are an unctuous warm-up to pasta, but can also double as finger food. We've included a traditional green salad—Boston lettuce with honey mustard and herbs—as well as richer options, like a luxuriously creamy quiche Lorraine. No matter when you decide to serve them, you'll be off to a great start.

Salt and Pepper Shrimp

MAKES ABOUT 25 HORS D'OEUVRES
Active time: 45 min   Start to finish: 45 min

In this shrimp dish (a staple on Sichuan menus) the shells and tails stay virtually intact—only a few snippets are removed. When deep-fried, the shells are transformed into a layer of pleasing crunch and crackle (a bit like soft-shelled crab).

1   lb large shrimp in their shells
    (about 25)
6   cups vegetable oil
¾   teaspoon fine sea salt
½   teaspoon Chinese five-spice powder

Special equipment: a deep-fat thermometer

Cut each shrimp shell lengthwise along back with scissors, leaving last segment intact, then devein shrimp, leaving shell in place. Cut off feathery legs and sharp pointed section of shell above soft tail fins. Rinse shrimp and dry thoroughly.

Heat oil in a wok or deep heavy pot over high heat until it registers 400°F on thermometer. Fry shrimp in 4 batches until shells bubble and shrimp are bright pink, 45 to 60 seconds (they will be slightly undercooked), transferring with a slotted spoon to paper towels to drain and returning oil to 400°F between batches. Carefully pour oil into a heatproof bowl (to cool before discarding). Wipe wok clean with paper towels.

Stir together sea salt, ½ teaspoon black pepper, and five-spice powder. Heat wok or a heavy skillet over moderate heat until hot but not smoking, then stir-fry deep-fried shrimp with spice mix 10 seconds. Serve immediately.

Potatoes Topped with Smoked Salmon and Fennel

MAKES 24 HORS D'OEUVRES
Active time: 15 min   Start to finish: 1½ hr

12   small (1½-inch) red boiling potatoes
2   oz smoked salmon, coarsely chopped
¼   cup finely chopped fennel bulb
     (sometimes called anise)
1   teaspoon fresh lemon juice
¼   cup low-fat sour cream

Garnish: fennel fronds or fresh dill sprigs

Cover potatoes with salted cold water by 1 inch in a large saucepan, then simmer, uncovered, until just tender, about 15 minutes. Drain in a colander and cool.

Stir together salmon, fennel, lemon juice, and salt and black pepper to taste.

Halve cooled potatoes and season cut sides with salt and black pepper, then arrange, cut sides up, on a platter (if potatoes wobble, cut a thin slice off rounded bottoms). Dot each with ½ teaspoon sour cream and mound salmon on top.

Cooks' notes:
• Potatoes can be cooked 3 hours ahead and kept, covered, at room temperature.
• Salmon topping can be made 3 hours ahead and chilled, covered.

Tuna Empanaditas

MAKES ABOUT 60 HORS D'OEUVRES
Active time: 1 hr   Start to finish: 1½ hr

Americans may not depend on tapas the way Spaniards do—to assuage hunger in the hours before a ten o'clock dinner—but these authentic tuna empanaditas *can become addictive. They're tasty, lightly satisfying, and just the right size for picking up with your fingers.*

1 (6-oz) can light tuna in olive oil (not drained)
½ cup finely chopped onion
½ cup finely chopped pimiento-stuffed green olives (3 oz), drained
2 tablespoons drained bottled capers, rinsed and chopped
1 (17¼-oz) package frozen puff pastry sheets, thawed

Special equipment: a 2¼-inch round cookie cutter

Preheat oven to 400°F.

Pour oil from tuna into a skillet, then add onion and cook over moderate heat, stirring occasionally, until softened, 3 to 4 minutes.

Mash tuna in a bowl with a fork, then stir in onion, olives, and capers. Season generously with black pepper and very lightly with salt.

Roll out 1 pastry sheet on a lightly floured surface with a lightly floured rolling pin into a 13-inch square. Cut out 30 rounds with floured cookie cutter and discard scraps.

Put ½ teaspoon tuna mixture in center of each pastry round. Hold 1 filled round in palm of your hand, then moisten edge with a finger dipped in water. Cup hand, then fold dough over to form a half-moon, pinching edges to seal (this creates a border for crimping). Transfer *empanadita* to an ungreased large baking sheet and form more with remaining rounds.

Press back of a fork onto border of each *empanadita* to crimp, then bake in batches in middle of oven until golden, 20 to 25 minutes. While *empanaditas* bake, make more with remaining pastry sheet and filling. Cool on baking sheet on a rack 10 minutes. Serve warm.

Cooks' note:
• *Empanaditas* can be formed (but not baked) 1 week ahead. Freeze in 1 layer in a shallow baking pan, then transfer to sealed plastic bags and keep frozen. Bake frozen *empanaditas* about 30 minutes.

Pistachio Twists

MAKES 40 HORS D'OEUVRES
Active time: 30 min   Start to finish: 45 min

1 (17¼-oz package) frozen puff pastry
   sheets, thawed
1 large egg, lightly beaten with
   2 teaspoons water
   Coarse salt for sprinkling
1 cup shelled unsalted pistachios
   (not dyed red), lightly toasted and
   finely chopped

Preheat oven to 425°F.

Roll out 1 pastry sheet, keeping remaining sheet covered and chilled, on a lightly floured surface with a lightly floured rolling pin into an 18- by 12-inch rectangle. Brush pastry with some egg wash and sprinkle lightly with coarse salt and black pepper to taste. With a short side of pastry facing you, sprinkle ½ cup nuts over lower half and press lightly into pastry with a rolling pin. Fold plain half of pastry over nuts to form a 12- by 9-inch rectangle, then firmly roll pin over pastry to force out any air pockets and to make layers adhere. Brush with some remaining egg wash and sprinkle lightly with more salt.

Cut pastry crosswise into ½-inch-wide strips with a pastry wheel or sharp knife. Transfer strips 1 at a time (1 inch apart) to 2 greased large baking sheets, twisting each strip about 3 to 4 times to enclose nuts and pressing both ends of each strip onto baking sheet.

Bake twists in batches in middle of oven until golden, 12 to 15 minutes. Make more in the same manner with remaining pastry sheet.

Anchovy Puffs

MAKES ABOUT 24 HORS D'OEUVRES
Active time: 10 min   Start to finish: 25 min

1 (2-oz) can flat anchovies, rinsed, patted
   dry, and minced
3 tablespoons mayonnaise
1 (17¼-oz package) frozen puff pastry
   sheets, thawed
1 large egg, lightly beaten with
   1 tablespoon water

Special equipment: a 3-inch decorative cookie cutter (preferably a fish shape)

Preheat oven to 375°F.

Mash together anchovies and mayonnaise in a small bowl with a fork. Roll out pastry sheets on a lightly floured surface into 14-inch squares, then trim edges to form 13-inch squares. Brush off any excess flour and spread anchovy mayonnaise evenly over 1 pastry sheet, leaving a ½-inch border. Cover with remaining pastry sheet and press sheets together gently.

Cut pastry into shapes with cookie cutter. Cut scraps into bite-size pieces to bake separately.

Arrange pastries on lightly greased baking sheets and brush tops with egg wash. Lightly score pastries with the edge of cookie cutter or back of a sharp knife. Bake pastries in upper and lower thirds of oven until puffed and golden, 12 to 15 minutes.

Prosciutto and Gruyère Pinwheels

MAKES ABOUT 40 HORS D'OEUVRES
Active time: 25 min   Start to finish: 4 hr

¾ cup finely grated Gruyère (3 oz)
4 teaspoons chopped fresh sage
1 frozen puff pastry sheet (from a
   17¼-oz package), thawed
1 large egg, lightly beaten
2 oz thinly sliced prosciutto

Preheat oven to 400°F.

Stir together Gruyère and sage in a bowl. Arrange pastry on a lightly floured surface with a short side nearest you and cut in half crosswise. Arrange 1 half with a long side nearest you and brush edge of far side with some egg. Arrange half of prosciutto evenly over pastry, avoiding egg-brushed edge, then sprinkle with half of Gruyère. Starting with side nearest you, roll pastry jelly-roll fashion into a log and wrap in wax paper. Make another log in same manner. Chill pastry logs, seam sides down, until firm, at least 3 hours.

Cut logs crosswise into ½-inch-thick slices and arrange about 1 inch apart on 2 lightly greased large baking sheets. Bake pinwheels in batches in middle of oven until golden, 14 to 16 minutes. Transfer to a rack to cool slightly. Serve warm.

Cooks' note:
• Pastry logs can be rolled, but not cut, and kept chilled up to 3 days.

Parmesan Garlic Sticks

MAKES ABOUT 36 HORS D'OEUVRES
Active time: 20 min   Start to finish: 40 min

½ stick (¼ cup) unsalted butter, cut
   into bits
½ cup all-purpose flour
3 large eggs
1 tablespoon minced garlic
¾ cup freshly grated parmesan

Special equipment: a pastry bag fitted with a ⅜-inch plain tip

Preheat oven to 425°F.

Bring ½ cup water and butter to a boil in a 2 quart saucepan over high heat, then reduce heat to low. Add flour all at once and beat mixture with a wooden spoon until it leaves side of pan and forms a ball. Transfer to a bowl, then beat in 2 eggs, 1 at a time, with an electric mixer at high speed, beating well after each addition. Dough should just fall from a spoon: If it's too stiff, lightly beat remaining egg in a small bowl and add just enough to dough to thin to proper consistency. Mash together garlic and ½ teaspoon salt with flat side of large heavy knife to form a paste, then stir into dough with parmesan.

Transfer dough to pastry bag and pipe 3-inch-long sticks about 2 inches apart onto 2 buttered baking sheets. Bake sticks in batches in middle of oven until puffed and crisp, 18 to 20 minutes, then transfer to racks to cool. Serve warm or at room temperature.

Pecan Blue Cheese Crackers

MAKES ABOUT 90 HORS D'OEUVRES
Active time: 20 min   Start to finish: 1 hr

1½ cups pecan halves
1 stick (½ cup) unsalted butter, softened
½ lb blue cheese, softened
1 large egg, separated
1 cup all-purpose flour

Preheat oven to 350°F.

Toast ½ cup pecans on a baking sheet in oven until a shade darker, about 7 minutes, then cool. Finely chop toasted pecans. Cream butter and cheese in a bowl with a fork until smooth. Add yolk, stirring until combined well. Add flour and chopped pecans and stir until mixture just forms a dough.

Halve dough and form each half into a 12- by 1¼-inch log on separate sheets of wax paper, using paper as a guide. Freeze logs, wrapped in wax paper, just until firm, about 30 minutes.

Cut logs crosswise into ¼-inch-thick slices and arrange about ½ inch apart on 2 lightly greased baking sheets. Top each cracker with a remaining pecan half, pressing slightly into dough. Brush tops of crackers, including pecans, with lightly beaten egg white.

Bake crackers in batches in upper and lower thirds of oven, switching position of sheets halfway through baking, until golden brown, about 15 minutes total.

Transfer crackers with a spatula to paper towels to absorb excess oil, then transfer to a rack to cool.

Quiche Lorraine

SERVES 6
Active time: 15 min   Start to finish: 1 hr

6 oz sliced bacon, chopped
3 large eggs
¾ cup heavy cream
6 oz grated Gruyère (3 cups)
1 (9-inch) pie shell (store-bought), thawed if frozen

Preheat oven to 425°F.

Cook chopped bacon in a 12-inch skillet over moderately high heat, stirring occasionally, until crisp, about 5 minutes, and transfer with a slotted spoon to paper towels to drain.

Whisk together eggs, cream, and ¼ teaspoon black pepper. Sprinkle bacon and cheese in bottom of pie shell, then pour custard into shell.

Put pie on a baking sheet and bake until top is just golden, about 10 minutes. Reduce oven temperature to 325°F and cook until set and puffed, 20 to 25 minutes. Transfer to a rack to cool slightly. Serve warm.

Jalapeño Cheddar Toasts

MAKES 8 TOASTS
Active time: 12 min   Start to finish: 15 min

8   oz grated extra-sharp Cheddar (2 cups)
½   cup mayonnaise
1½   tablespoons minced pickled jalapeños,
**   drained**
8   slices firm white or whole-wheat
**   sandwich bread**

Preheat broiler.

Stir together Cheddar cheese, mayonnaise, and jalapeños.

Arrange bread slices on a large baking sheet and broil about 3 inches from heat until lightly toasted, 30 seconds to 1 minute per side. Divide cheese mayonnaise among slices, spreading evenly, then broil until slightly puffed and golden, about 1 minute. Serve immediately.

Slow-Roasted Tomatoes

SERVES 4 TO 6
Active time: 15 min   Start to finish: 6 hr

4   lb plum tomatoes, halved lengthwise
6   garlic cloves, minced
5   tablespoons extra-virgin olive oil plus
**   additional for drizzling**

Accompaniment: toasted baguette slices

Preheat oven to 200°F.

Put tomatoes, cut sides up, in 2 large shallow baking pans. Stir together garlic and oil and spoon over tomatoes, then season with salt and black pepper. Roast in oven 6 to 8 hours (tomatoes will be reduced in size but will retain their shape). Cool to room temperature.

Serve tomatoes on toasts, drizzled with additional oil.

Cooks' note:
• Roasted tomatoes keep, chilled in an airtight container, 2 weeks. Bring to room temperature before using.

Potato Latkes

MAKES 12 TO 16 LATKES
Active time: 45 min   Start to finish: 45 min

What is the secret to making great latkes? We found that the starchier the potato, the crisper the latke. As for varieties, we tested baking potatoes (the starchiest), Yukon Golds, and boiling potatoes (the least starchy) and liked them all. You can easily double this recipe for a crowd.

- **1   lb potatoes**
- **½   cup finely chopped onion**
- **1   large egg, lightly beaten**
- **½   to ¾ cup olive oil**

Accompaniments: sour cream
       and applesauce

Preheat oven to 250°F.

Peel potatoes and coarsely grate by hand, transferring to a large bowl of cold water. Soak potatoes 1 to 2 minutes after last batch is added to water, then drain well in a colander.

Spread grated potatoes and onion on a kitchen towel, then roll up jelly-roll style and twist towel tightly to wring out as much liquid as possible. Transfer potato and onion to a bowl and stir in egg and ½ teaspoon salt.

Heat ¼ cup oil in a 12-inch nonstick skillet over moderately high heat until hot but not smoking. Working in batches of 4 latkes, spoon 2 tablespoons potato mixture per latke into skillet, spreading into 3-inch rounds with a fork. Reduce heat to moderate and cook until undersides are browned, about 5 minutes. Turn latkes over and cook until undersides are browned, about 5 minutes more. Transfer to paper towels to drain and season with salt. Add more oil to skillet as needed. Keep latkes warm in oven on a rack set in a shallow baking pan.

Cooks' notes:
- Latkes can be made 2 hours ahead and kept at room temperature. Reheat on a rack set in a shallow baking pan in a 350°F oven, about 5 minutes.
- Grating the potatoes, soaking them briefly in water, and then squeezing out the liquid keeps the batter from turning brown too quickly.

Two-Bean Salad

SERVES 4
Active time: 15 min   Start to finish: 20 min

2   tablespoons Sherry vinegar
¼   cup extra-virgin olive oil
¾   lb green beans, trimmed and cut
      into 1-inch pieces
1   shallot, thinly sliced
1   (19-oz) can *cannellini* beans,
      drained and rinsed

Whisk together vinegar, oil, ¼ teaspoon salt, and ⅛ teaspoon black pepper in a large bowl.

Cook green beans in a 3- to 4-quart saucepan of boiling salted water 2 minutes, then add shallot and cook until beans are crisp-tender, about 2 minutes more. Drain in a large colander and plunge into a large bowl of ice and cold water to stop cooking, then drain well. Toss vegetables and *cannellini* beans with dressing in bowl.

Roasted Pepper Salad

SERVES 4
Active time: 20 min   Start to finish: 45 min

4   assorted bell peppers (preferably red,
      yellow, and orange)
2   teaspoons balsamic vinegar
2   teaspoons chopped fresh thyme
1   tablespoon drained bottled capers,
      coarsely chopped
1   bunch arugula (¼ lb), tough stems
      discarded

Roast peppers on racks of gas burners over high heat, turning with tongs, until skins are blackened, 10 to 12 minutes. (Or broil peppers in a broiler pan about 5 inches from heat, turning occasionally, about 15 minutes.) Transfer to a bowl and let stand, covered, until cool enough to handle.

Peel peppers over bowl (to catch any liquid) and discard stems and seeds. Cut peppers lengthwise into 1-inch-thick strips and add to liquid in bowl, then toss with vinegar, thyme, capers, and salt and black pepper to taste.

Divide arugula among serving plates. Top with peppers and drizzle with any remaining dressing. Serve at room temperature or chilled.

Cooks' note:
• Dressed peppers can be made 3 days ahead and chilled, covered.

Daikon Ginger Salad

SERVES 4 (LIGHT STARTER OR SIDE DISH)
Active time: 15 min   Start to finish: 15 min

- **1 lb piece daikon radish, peeled**
- **1 large carrot**
- **3 tablespoons seasoned rice vinegar**
- **1 tablespoon finely grated peeled fresh ginger**
- **3 tablespoons coarsely chopped fresh cilantro**

Shred radish and carrot using medium shredding disk of a food processor or tear-drop-shaped holes on a box grater.

Stir together vinegar and ginger in a bowl, then add radish, carrot, and cilantro and toss to combine.

Cooks' note:

- Salad can be made 3 hours ahead and chilled, covered.

Boston Lettuce Salad with Honey Mustard and Herbs

SERVES 2 TO 4
Active time: 10 min   Start to finish: 10 min

- **1½ tablespoons honey mustard**
- **2 tablespoons mild olive oil**
- **1 (½-lb) head Boston lettuce, leaves torn into bite-size pieces**
- **1 teaspoon finely chopped fresh tarragon**
- **1 tablespoon finely chopped fresh chive**

Whisk together mustard, oil, 2 teaspoons water, and salt and black pepper to taste, then toss with lettuce, tarragon, and chive in a salad bowl.

Gone are the days when a salad meant a wedge of lettuce accessorized with a blob of bottled dressing. Now shopping for greens can be downright daunting. When you start with stuff that's just been picked, though, it's pretty hard to get it wrong. Quality olive oil and good salt alone will make your salad sing, but you might also try a rice vinegar to bring out the sweetness in your greens, a balsamic for something extra rich, or a fruit vinegar to dress strong herbs. A nutty oil will add depth, and colorful blossoms will brighten a background of green. My favorite light and neutral oil is grapeseed.

dressing a green salad

The traditional balance for a vinaigrette is one part acid to three parts oil, but if the dressing is sweet, the proportion can go as low as one to one (good for low-fat salads). To cut the acid, add shallots, as they do in France, or more oil, salt, or sugar. Add mustard to help with emulsification and to balance the oil and acid. Oil stirred into Dijon mustard (no vinegar necessary) is a French classic. —SHELTON WISEMAN

ALCOHOLIC

Frozen Mango Daiquiris **30**

Guava Batidas **29**

Irish Mocha Frosts **30**

Peach Gin Freezes **30**

Peach Sangría **29**

Tamarind Margarita **29**

NON-ALCOHOLIC

Apricot Iced Tea **32**

Ginger Iced Tea **32**

Coffee Avocado Milkshakes **30**

Cranberry Pineapple Punch **32**

Rhubarb Mint Coolers **33**

Sparkling Mango Limeade **33**

Cool Drinks

nothing says "refreshing" like the sound of ice cubes clinking in a glass or the whir of a blender mixing up tropical drinks. In true *Gourmet* style, we've taken some classics and added our own twists. Limeade blended with mangoes and topped off with club soda becomes an exotic sparkling treat. Tired of heavy red wine sangría with floating orange and apple chunks? Our peach sangría, made with a lighter rosé and peach slices, is as beautiful as it is delicious. We even put an icy spin on a hot ol' favorite with our cool version of Irish coffee—Irish mocha frosts.

peach sangria

Peach Sangría

MAKES 4 DRINKS
Active time: 10 min   Start to finish: 1¼ hr

2 firm-ripe peaches, cut into thin wedges
½ cup peach schnapps
⅓ cup superfine granulated sugar
**3 cups rosé wine (from a 750-ml bottle),
    chilled**
2 cups sparkling water, chilled

Stir together peaches, schnapps, and sugar in a large pitcher until sugar is dissolved and let stand 1 hour.
Stir in wine, sparkling water, and some ice.

Guava Batidas

MAKES ABOUT 6 DRINKS
Active time: 8 min   Start to finish: 8 min

**3 (12-oz) cans guava nectar
    (preferably Goya)**
**¾ cup Brazilian Cachaça
    (cane sugar liquor)**
2 to 3 tablespoons lime juice
**   Ice cubes**

Stir together guava nectar, Cachaça, and lime juice in a pitcher, then fill with ice. Serve in small tumblers.

Cooks' note:
• For a frozen batida, blend all ingredients with ice until smooth.

Tamarind Margarita

MAKES 1 DRINK
Active time: 3 min   Start to finish: 3 min

½ lime
**   Kosher salt for rim**
**   Ice cubes**
1½ oz Tequila (preferably Reposado)
¾ cup tamarind nectar (from a 12-oz can)

Garnish: lime slice

Rub lime half around rim of a 12-oz tumbler, then dip rim in a plate of kosher salt. Fill tumbler with ice and squeeze 1 teaspoon juice from lime half into tumbler. Stir in Tequila and nectar.

Tamarind is perhaps the ultimate fusion ingredient; its complex fruity-sour quality is indispensable in the cuisines of India, Southeast Asia, the Caribbean, and Latin America. For our tamarind margarita we used canned tamarind juice, since you can find it in your supermarket under the Goya brand. And rather than fussing with the pressed pulp, we often use the concentrate, which comes in a jar (and is available at specialty food shops). The concentrate is wonderful in the long, tall Mexican cooler called *tamarindo*: Whiz up 1 tablespoon concentrate, 2 to 3 tablespoons sugar, and ⅓ cup water in a blender until smooth, then blend in ⅔ cup water. Serve over ice.

—JANE DANIELS LEAR

Frozen Mango Daiquiris

MAKES 2 DRINKS
Active time: 5 min   Start to finish: 5 min

1 ripe mango, peeled and chopped (1 cup)
3 oz dark rum (6 tablespoons)
1 tablespoon sugar
2 teaspoons fresh lime juice
2 cups cracked ice

Blend all ingredients in a blender, scraping down side occasionally, until smooth but still frozen.

Serve daiquiris in 2 stemmed glasses.

Irish Mocha Frosts

MAKES 2 DRINKS
Active time: 10 min   Start to finish: 3 hr

½ cup freshly brewed strong coffee
1 cup milk
4 teaspoons unsweetened cocoa powder
1 cup cream whiskey liqueur such as
   Bailey's Irish Cream, chilled

Heat coffee, milk, and cocoa in a small saucepan over moderate heat, whisking, until cocoa is dissolved. Remove from heat and cool.

Stir in ½ cup liqueur. Pour mixture into an ice tray and freeze until frozen solid, about 3 hours. Blend frozen coffee cubes in a blender with remaining ½ cup liqueur, scraping down side occasionally, until smooth but still frozen.

Serve frosts in 2 stemmed glasses.

Cooks' note:
• Coffee cubes can be frozen 1 day ahead.

Peach Gin Freezes

MAKES 2 DRINKS
Active time: 5 min   Start to finish: 5 min

1½ cups peach nectar
4½ oz gin (9 tablespoons)
1½ oz peach schnapps (3 tablespoons)
3 cups cracked ice

Blend all ingredients in a blender, scraping down side occasionally, until smooth but still frozen.

Serve gin freezes in 2 stemmed glasses.

Coffee Avocado Milkshakes

MAKES 2 SHAKES
Active time: 15 min   Start to finish: 15 min

This recipe is inspired by es alpukat, *a delicious, refreshing Indonesian coffee drink, that gets its richness and body from avocado. Traditionally it is served over ice, but we prefer the ice blended in.*

½ ripe large California avocado
⅓ cup espresso or 1 cup strong
   brewed coffee, cooled
½ cup sweetened condensed
   (not evaporated) milk
2 cups ice cubes
2 teaspoons vanilla

Scoop avocado flesh into a blender, then purée with remaining ingredients until completely smooth, about 1 minute.

Cooks' note:
• If you have a large (6-cup) blender, you can double this recipe and still make it in 1 batch.

coffee avocado milkshakes

Ginger Iced Tea

¼ cup sliced peeled fresh ginger
      (about a 2½- by 1½-inch piece)
4 oolong tea bags
½ cup simple syrup plus 1 tablespoon, or
      to taste (recipe below), chilled

Bring 4 cups water and ginger just to a boil and pour over tea bags in a 1-quart glass measure or heatproof bowl. Steep 5 minutes, then remove tea bags and steep ginger 1½ hours more. Pour tea through a fine sieve into a pitcher. Chill, covered, until cold, about 1 hour.

Stir in simple syrup and serve tea over ice in tall glasses.

Simple Syrup

MAKES ABOUT 2 CUPS
Active time: 5 min   Start to finish: 2 hr

1⅓ cups sugar

Boil sugar and 1¼ cups water in a saucepan, stirring, until sugar is completely dissolved. Cool syrup to room temperature, then chill, covered.

Cooks' note:
• Syrup can be made 2 weeks ahead and chilled, covered.

Apricot Iced Tea

MAKES 8 DRINKS
Active time: 5 min   Start to finish: 1¼ hr

3 orange pekoe tea bags
5 (5½-oz) cans apricot nectar
      (3⅓ cups), chilled
½ cup simple syrup, or to taste
      (recipe this page), chilled

Bring 4 cups water just to a boil and pour over tea bags in a heatproof pitcher. Steep 5 minutes, then remove tea bags and cool to room temperature. Chill, covered, until cold, about 1 hour.

Stir in nectar and syrup and serve tea over ice in tall glasses.

Cranberry Pineapple Punch

MAKES ABOUT 26 DRINKS
Active time: 5 min   Start to finish: 5 min

2 (1-qt) bottles cranberry juice cocktail,
      chilled
1 (46-oz) can unsweetened pineapple
      juice, chilled
2 cups ginger ale, chilled
2 cups seltzer water, chilled
2 trays ice

Garnish: fresh pineapple spears

Stir together juices, ginger ale, and seltzer water in a large punch bowl, then add ice.

Sparkling Mango Limeade

MAKES 6 DRINKS
Active time: 10 min   Start to finish: 1 hr

**3   ripe mangoes (2½ lb total),
     peeled and pitted**
1½ cups fresh lime juice
**1   cup superfine sugar plus additional
     Seltzer or club soda, chilled**

Garnish: lime wedges

Blend mangoes, lime juice, 1 cup sugar, and
1½ cups water in a blender until smooth, then
force through a sieve into a pitcher, pressing on
and discarding any solids. Chill purée, covered,
until cold, about 1 hour. (Purée will be slightly
thick). Stir in additional sugar to taste.

Fill tall glasses with ice and fill each glass
three quarters full with purée. Top off with seltzer
and stir well.

Cooks' note:
• Limeade purée keeps 2 days, covered and
  chilled.

Rhubarb Mint Coolers

MAKES ABOUT 6 DRINKS
Active time: 5 min   Start to finish: 3½ hr

*Although most people think of rhubarb as a fruit,
it's actually a vegetable that's available from
April through June. Fresh stalks shouldn't be
rubbery—they should snap in half when bent.*

**1   lb rhubarb, trimmed and cut into
     ½ inch pieces**
1   cup sugar
¼   cup fresh mint leaves

Garnish: fresh mint sprigs

Bring rhubarb, sugar, mint leaves, and 5 cups
water to a boil in a saucepan, then simmer,
stirring occasionally, 15 minutes (rhubarb will
disintegrate). Cool 15 minutes, then pour through
a fine sieve into a pitcher, pressing hard on and
discarding solids. Chill, covered, until cold, about
3 hours.

Serve over ice in glasses.

Cooks' note:
• Rhubarb mint coolers keep 2 days, covered
  and chilled.

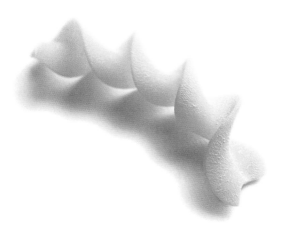

Pasta

With myriad pasta shapes and so many flavorful ingredients and sauce combinations, our cooks went wild with this chapter. Orecchiette, paired with broccoli rabe and creamy garlic Gorgonzola sauce, is a taste and texture masterpiece. Gemelli, tossed with a simple pumpkin purée, becomes a dish that tastes far more intricate than its five little ingredients. And then there's homemade potato gnocchi with brown butter and sage; tarragon lime bay scallops over angel-hair pasta; or rotini with cabbage and kielbasa, too. But don't worry, we haven't forgotten about the dishes that say "home." In fact, we've given extra-special attention to comfort-food favorites like mac' and cheese and spaghetti with meat sauce.

Baked Macaroni and Cheese with Stewed Tomatoes

SERVES 4
Active time: 15 min   Start to finish: 1¼ hr

½ lb elbow macaroni
1 (14- to 15-oz) can diced stewed tomatoes
¾ cup heavy cream
3 cups coarsely grated extra-sharp
    Cheddar (½ lb)

Preheat oven to 400°F.

Cook macaroni in a large pot of boiling salted water until tender, then drain in a colander.

Toss macaroni, tomatoes, cream, 2 cups cheese, ½ teaspoon salt, and ¼ teaspoon black pepper in a 2-quart shallow baking dish, then sprinkle remaining cup cheese over top. Bake in middle of oven until juices are absorbed and top is golden brown, about 45 minutes.

Pasta with Pancetta and Peas

SERVES 4
Active time: 15 min Start to finish: 15 min

¼ cup extra-virgin olive oil
1 large onion, chopped
¼ lb sliced pancetta, chopped
1 (10-oz) package frozen peas,
    thawed (2 cups)
¾ lb linguine fini or spaghetti

Heat oil in a 12-inch skillet over moderately high heat until hot but not smoking, then cook onion until golden brown, about 5 minutes. Add pancetta and cook until browned and crisp, 3 to 5 minutes. Reduce heat to moderate, then stir in peas, 1 teaspoon salt, and ½ teaspoon black pepper and cook until peas are heated through, about 1 minute. Remove from heat.

Cook pasta in a 6- to 8-quart pot of boiling salted water until al dente. Reserve 1 cup cooking water, then drain pasta in a colander and transfer to a serving bowl. Add reserved pasta water to skillet and deglaze by simmering, stirring and scraping up browned bits, 1 minute, then add to pasta with pancetta and peas and toss to combine.

garlic

It turns out that garlic is as common and universal as a handshake—albeit a hearty one. Not only is it a staple in Mediterranean dishes, it's used in cuisines all over the world from Africa, China, Mexico to the West Indies. And because of global recipe swapping, garlic has become a comfort food in its own right.

There are two main varieties—**softnecks,** the ubiquitous type sold at local supermarkets, whose cloves grow in layers like the leaves of an artichoke — and the more flavorful **hardnecks,** which can be identified by the stick peeking out from the middle and usually one ring of cloves surrounding it. The papery skin on both types can vary from bright white, to off-white, to even white streaked with red or purple (not to be confused with milder elephant garlic— those enormous purple bulbs actually belong to the leek family). When purchasing garlic, choose bulbs that are firm with cloves that are full (not shrunk away from their skin). Bulbs that have green shoots peeking out are too old.

Although garlic is available all-year round, look for fresh locally grown garlic, typically harvested in late summer. Fresh garlic, if properly stored, can keep for months, but most bulbs purchased from supermarkets have already been stored for quite some time, so once you get them home they won't last long. To stave off their demise, keep bulbs in a cool, dry, dark place, preferably in a container that allows air to circulate around them, like a wire basket or porous terracotta pot. DO NOT refrigerate, this dehydrates cloves and causes the garlic to loose flavor.

And as far as flavor goes, garlic has multiple personalities, depending on how it's treated. In its raw state it's at its most intense. Cooking garlic until soft but not colored mellows it, to an almost sweet creaminess, while browning it lends a nutty flavor to foods. —LINDA IMMEDIATO

Cheese Ravioli
with Tomato-Olive Sauce

SERVES 4
Active time: 10 min   Start to finish: 30 min

1 (28- to 32-oz) can crushed tomatoes
3 garlic cloves, minced
¼ cup finely chopped Kalamata or
**   other brine-cured black olives**
3 tablespoons fresh orange juice,
**   or to taste**
1½ lb frozen cheese ravioli or tortellini

Simmer tomatoes, garlic, and olives in a
3-quart heavy saucepan, uncovered, stirring
occasionally, until slightly thickened,
10 to 15 minutes. Remove from heat and stir
in orange juice and salt and black pepper to
taste and keep warm, covered.

Cook pasta in a 6- to 8- quart pot of boiling
salted water until tender and drain in a colander.

Serve immediately, topped with sauce.

Spaghetti with Meat Sauce

SERVES 4
Active time: 25 min   Start to finish: 25 min

1½ lb ground beef chuck (not lean)
1 large garlic clove, finely chopped
1 (28-oz) can whole plum tomatoes
**   in juice**
¾ lb spaghetti
2½ oz freshly grated parmesan (¾ cup)

Brown beef in a 4- to 5-quart heavy saucepan
over moderately high heat, stirring and breaking
up lumps, then transfer with a slotted spoon
to a bowl.

Pour off all but 1 tablespoon fat from pan, then
cook garlic in fat remaining in pan over moderate
heat, stirring, until golden. Add tomatoes with
juice and simmer sauce, uncovered, stirring
occasionally and breaking up tomatoes, until
reduced to about 2 cups, 12 to 15 minutes. Stir
in beef with any juices accumulated in bowl and
season with salt and black pepper.

While sauce is simmering, cook pasta in a
large pot of boiling salted water until al dente,
then drain in a colander. Add pasta to meat sauce
and toss to combine.

Serve pasta sprinkled with parmesan.

Linguine with Scallion Sauce and Sautéed Shrimp

SERVES 4
Active time: 30 min   Start to finish: 50 min

¾ **lb scallions (3 large bunches)**
6 **to 7 tablespoons olive oil**
2 **garlic cloves, minced**
1 **lb medium shrimp (24), shelled
    and deveined**
1 **lb dried linguine**

Garnish: thinly sliced scallion greens

Cut enough scallion greens into 2-inch pieces to measure 3 cups and finely chop white parts.

Cook finely chopped white parts of scallions in 2 tablespoons oil in a deep 12-inch heavy skillet over moderately low heat, stirring, until tender, about 5 minutes. Add garlic and cook, stirring, 1 minute. Transfer garlic and scallions to a blender and wipe skillet clean.

Blanch scallion greens in a large pot of boiling salted water 30 seconds, then transfer to blender with a slotted spoon. Transfer ¼ cup scallion cooking water to blender and keep water remaining in pot over low heat, covered. Blend scallion mixture with 2 tablespoons oil until smooth (use caution when blending hot liquids) and season sauce with salt and black pepper.

Heat 2 tablespoons oil in skillet over moderately high heat until hot but not smoking, then sauté half of shrimp, turning them, until golden brown and just cooked through, about 2 minutes. Transfer to a plate and keep warm, covered. Sauté remaining shrimp in same manner, adding remaining tablespoon oil if necessary.

Return water in pot to a boil and cook pasta, stirring occasionally, until al dente. Reserve 1 cup pasta water and drain pasta in a colander. Add pasta to skillet with sauce and ¼ cup pasta water and heat over low heat, gently tossing and adding more pasta water as needed, until just heated through.

Serve pasta with shrimp.

Gemelli with Pumpkin Sauce

SERVES 4 TO 6
Active time: 10 min   Start to finish: 25 min

2 **tablespoons unsalted butter**
1 **medium onion, finely chopped**
1⅓ **cups canned pumpkin purée**
1 **lb *gemelli***
⅓ **cup grated parmesan (1 oz), plus
    additional for serving**

Heat butter in a 2-quart saucepan over moderate heat until foam subsides, then cook onion, stirring frequently, until golden brown, 6 to 8 minutes. Stir in pumpkin purée, 2 teaspoons salt, and ½ teaspoon black pepper and remove from heat.

Cook *gemelli* in a 6- to 8-quart pot of boiling salted water until al dente. Reserve 1½ cups cooking water, then drain pasta in a colander. Return pasta to pot and toss with pumpkin sauce and reserved cooking water, then stir in cheese.

Fettuccine with Sautéed Zucchini

SERVES 4
Active time: 20 min   Start to finish: 25 min

1½ lb medium zucchini (3), trimmed,
    quartered lengthwise, and seeded
¼   cup extra-virgin olive oil
2   large garlic cloves, minced
½   lb egg fettuccine (in nests)
½   cup finely grated Parmigiano-Reggiano

Cut zucchini spears in 3-inch lengths, then cut lengthwise into ¼-inch julienne strips. Heat oil in a 12-inch heavy skillet over high heat until hot but not smoking, then sauté zucchini strips, stirring, until golden, about 8 minutes. Add garlic and 1 teaspoon salt and sauté, stirring, until garlic is fragrant, 1 to 2 minutes.

Cook pasta in a large pot of boiling salted water until al dente. Reserve ½ cup cooking water, then drain pasta in a colander. Add pasta and reserved cooking water to zucchini, then toss with cheese and cook over moderate heat 1 to 2 minutes.

Tarragon Lime Bay Scallops over Angel-Hair Pasta

SERVES 4 GENEROUSLY
Active time: 20 min   Start to finish: 20 min

¾   lb dried angel-hair pasta
    (capelli d'angelo)
1½ lb bay scallops or quartered
    sea scallops, tough muscle removed
    from side of each if necessary
¾   stick (6 tablespoons) unsalted butter
3   tablespoons fresh lime juice, or to taste
2   tablespoons finely chopped fresh
    tarragon, or to taste

Cook pasta in a 6- to 8- quart pot of boiling salted water until al dente. Reserve ¼ cup cooking water, then drain pasta in a colander.

While pasta is cooking, pat scallops dry and season with salt and black pepper. Heat 3 tablespoons butter in a 12-inch nonstick skillet over moderately high heat until foam subsides, then cook half of scallops, stirring, until golden, about 3 minutes. Transfer with a slotted spoon to a bowl. Cook remaining scallops in remaining butter in same manner. Return scallops to skillet and stir in lime juice and tarragon.

Toss pasta in a bowl with half of scallops and ¼ cup pasta cooking liquid. Top pasta with remaining scallops and sauce and season with salt and black pepper.

Orecchiette with Broccoli Rabe and Gorgonzola Sauce

SERVES 4 TO 6
Active time: 15 min   Start to finish: 30 min

If the bitterness of broccoli rabe is too strong for your liking, substitute Broccolini, a broccoli hybrid that resembles rabe but has a sweet flavor.

- 1 lb broccoli rabe, trimmed and cut into 2-inch pieces
- ⅓ cup heavy cream
- 1 medium garlic clove, thinly sliced
- 7 oz Gorgonzola, crumbled
- 1 lb *orecchiette* (ear-shaped pasta)

Cook broccoli rabe in a 6- to 8-quart pot of boiling salted water until just tender, about 5 minutes. Transfer broccoli rabe with a slotted spoon to a colander to drain, reserving pot of boiling water for cooking pasta, then transfer to serving bowl.

Stir together cream and garlic in a small saucepan and cook at a bare simmer 2 minutes. Add Gorgonzola and whisk until melted, then season with ½ teaspoon salt and ½ teaspoon black pepper. Keep sauce warm, covered.

Cook *orecchiette* in reserved boiling water until al dente. Reserve 1 cup cooking water, then drain pasta in colander. Add ½ cup cooking water to Gorgozola sauce, then add pasta and sauce to broccoli rabe and toss to combine, adding more pasta water as necessary for desired consistency.

Orecchiette with Smoked Trout and Sugar Snap Peas

SERVES 4
Active time: 15 min   Start to finish: 30 min

- 1 lb *orecchiette* (ear-shaped pasta)
- 12 oz sugar snap peas, trimmed and halved diagonally
- ½ cup heavy cream
- 6 oz whole smoked trout, head, skin, bone, and tail discarded and flesh cut into 1-inch pieces
- 1 teaspoon finely grated fresh lemon zest

Cook pasta in a large pot of boiling salted water until al dente, 8 to 10 minutes. Add sugar snaps to water 2 minutes before pasta is done cooking. Reserve ½ cup cooking water, then drain pasta and sugar snaps in a colander. Transfer pasta and sugar snaps back to pot.

Simmer cream in a small saucepan 1 minute and remove from heat.

Add cream, trout, zest, and reserved cooking water to pasta and toss well.

Rotini with Cabbage and Kielbasa

SERVES 4
Active time: 15 min   Start to finish: 25 min

Cabbage mellows and sweetens when cooked. We combined it with kielbasa for a spicy-sweet combination that's surprisingly delicious.

- ¾ **lb kielbasa, coarsely chopped**
- 1 **lb green cabbage, thinly sliced (6 cups)**
- ½ **teaspoon dried hot red pepper flakes**
- ¾ **lb rotini**

Brown kielbasa in a 10- to 12-inch heavy skillet over moderately high heat, stirring, then transfer with a slotted spoon to a bowl.

Add cabbage to fat remaining in skillet and cook, stirring occasionally, until browned, about 6 minutes. (Skillet will be very full when cabbage is added, but cabbage will wilt as it cooks.) Stir in red pepper flakes and 1 cup water and cook, covered, over moderate heat until cabbage is tender, about 10 minutes. Stir in kielbasa.

While cabbage is cooking, cook pasta in a large pot of boiling salted water until al dente. Reserve 1 cup cooking water, then drain pasta in a colander.

Toss pasta with cabbage and salt to taste in pot, adding some of reserved cooking water to moisten if necessary.

Fettuccine with Arrabbiata Sauce

SERVES 4
Active time: 5 min   Start to finish: 30 min

Those who enjoy spicy sauces will want to try this one. Arrabbiata means "angry" in Italian and this sauce is certainly hot-tempered, especially when you add the maximum amount of red pepper flakes. And if you happen to have some around, freshly grated parmesan makes a great addition.

- ¼ **cup olive oil**
- 2 **garlic cloves, thinly sliced**
- ½ **to ¾ teaspoon dried hot red pepper flakes**
- 1 **(28-oz) can whole plum tomatoes with juice, coarsely chopped**
- ¾ **lb fettuccine**

Heat oil in a 5-quart saucepan over moderately high heat until hot but not smoking, then cook garlic and red pepper flakes (to taste), stirring, 2 minutes (do not brown). Stir in tomatoes with juice and salt and black pepper to taste. Reduce heat and simmer, stirring occasionally, until sauce is thickened, 20 to 25 minutes.

While sauce simmers, cook pasta in a large pot of boiling salted water until al dente. Drain pasta in a colander and return to pot. Toss pasta with sauce.

Potato and Onion Pierogis

SERVES 4 TO 6
Active time: 40 min   Start to finish: 40 min

1 lb boiling potatoes, peeled and cut
   into ½-inch pieces
1 large onion, chopped (1½ cups)
5 tablespoons unsalted butter
28 to 32 wonton wrappers, thawed
   if frozen
½ cup sour cream

Make filling:

Boil potatoes in cold salted water to cover by 1 inch in a 1-quart saucepan until tender, about 15 minutes, then drain well. Mash potatoes and cool.

While potatoes are boiling, cook onion in 4 tablespoons butter in a large heavy skillet over moderately low heat, stirring occasionally, until well browned, 10 to 12 minutes. Stir half of onion into mashed potatoes and season with salt and black pepper. Reserve remaining onion in skillet.

Make and cook pierogis:

Place 1 rounded teaspoon of filling in center of 1 wonton wrapper (keep remaining wrappers tightly covered with plastic wrap). Moisten edges of wrapper with water and fold in half to form a triangle, pressing down around filling to force out air, and press edges firmly together to seal. Transfer to a dry kitchen towel. Make more pierogis in same manner.

Briskly simmer pierogis in a 6-quart pot of salted water and cook, stirring once or twice, until tender, 2 to 3 minutes. Transfer pierogis to skillet with a slotted spoon and reserve ½ cup cooking water. Add remaining tablespoon butter to skillet and cook pierogis over low heat, stirring gently to coat with onions and adding enough reserved cooking water to moisten, until heated through.

Divide pierogis among plates and top with sour cream.

Cooks' note:
• Pierogis can be filled 1 day ahead and chilled, tightly wrapped on a kitchen towel-lined baking sheet. Bring to room temperature before cooking.

Potato Gnocchi with Brown Butter and Sage

SERVES 6
Active time: 30 min   Start to finish: 1 hr

1½ **lb boiling potatoes**
1½ **cups all-purpose flour**
  3 **tablespoons unsalted butter**
  1 **tablespoon chopped fresh sage**
⅓ **cup freshly grated Parmigiano-Reggiano**
     plus additional for serving

Special equipment: a food mill or ricer

Cover potatoes with salted cold water to cover by 2 inches in a large pot and simmer potatoes, covered, until tender, about 25 minutes. Drain potatoes and peel when cool enough to handle.

Force warm potatoes through food mill into a bowl, then add flour and 1¼ teaspoons salt and stir just until dough begins to come together. Gently press dough into a ball.

Halve ball and knead each half on a floured surface until smooth. Divide each half into 6 pieces, then roll each piece into a 10-inch-long rope (¾-inch thick). Cut each rope into ¾-inch pieces.

Press a piece of dough against tines of a floured fork and push with a floured thumb in a forward motion toward end of tines, letting gnocchi fall from fork onto floured kitchen towel. Repeat with remaining pieces of dough.

Cook gnocchi in 3 batches in a large pot of boiling salted water 1 minute, then transfer with a slotted spoon to a bowl.

Heat butter in a small saucepan over moderate heat until it turns golden brown. Remove from heat and toss gnocchi with butter, sage, cheese, and ¼ teaspoon black pepper. Serve with additional cheese.

Nobody ever said making the fluffy little dumplings called gnocchi (NYO-kee) was easy, exactly, but it's amazing what a delicate touch and a little practice can do. (If you have a knack with biscuits, you'll be good at this.) The most popular dough is made from potatoes and flour. Here are a few tips:
• Roll gnocchi dough into a rope very gently. If it's overhandled, the end result will be tough and heavy.
• If your knife begins to stick while you're cutting each rope into pieces, dip the blade into flour. • To form gnocchi, push with a floured thumb as you simultaneously roll a piece of dough against the curve of the fork tines. (You want to flick, not drag, the gnocchi off the fork.) —JANE DANIELS LEAR

Pasta with Asparagus-Lemon Sauce

SERVES 4

Active time: 35 min   Start to finish: 45 min

Faith Heller Willinger shared this recipe with us before it appeared in her Red, White & Greens: The Italian Way with Vegetables. *Ever since then, as soon as locally grown asparagus comes into season, this dish has been our rite of spring.*

Though penne is Faith's pasta of choice for this dish, we tried other types—such as mafalde *(similar to lasagna noodles but not quite as wide)—and found they work well, too.*

- **1 lb fresh asparagus, trimmed**
- **1 teaspoon finely grated fresh lemon zest**
- **¼ cup extra-virgin olive oil**
- **1 lb penne or other dried pasta**
- **½ cup freshly grated Parmigiano-Reggiano**

Cut asparagus into 1-inch pieces, reserving tips separately. Cook stems in 5 to 6 quarts boiling water with 2 tablespoons salt until very tender, 6 to 8 minutes. Transfer with a slotted spoon to a colander, reserving cooking water in pot, and rinse under cold water. Drain asparagus well and transfer to a food processor or blender.

Cook asparagus tips in same boiling water until just tender, 3 to 5 minutes. Transfer tips with slotted spoon to colander, reserving water in pot, and rinse under cold water. Drain tips well.

Purée asparagus stems with zest, oil, and ½ cup asparagus cooking water, then transfer sauce to a 4-quart saucepan.

Cook pasta in boiling asparagus cooking water until it still offers considerable resistance to the tooth, around three fourths of recommended cooking time. Reserve 2 cups cooking water and drain pasta.

Add pasta, asparagus tips, and ½ cup reserved pasta water to asparagus sauce and cook over high heat, stirring, 3 to 5 minutes, or until pasta is almost al dente and sauce coats pasta. Add more cooking water, ¼ cup at a time, until sauce coats pasta but is a little loose (the cheese will thicken it slightly).

Stir in Parmigiano-Reggiano and salt and black pepper to taste and cook, stirring, until cheese is melted. Serve immediately.

WHOLE BIRDS
Mustard Roasted Chicken **50**
Whole Roasted Chicken with Olives, Orange, and Thyme **53**
Roast Cornish Hens with Garlic-Sherry Vinegar Jus **52**
Braised Chicken with Shallots, Garlic, and Balsamic Vinegar **57**

BREASTS • CUTLETS • GROUND
Chicken Breasts with Spinach, Prosciutto, and Mozzarella **54**
Escallopes of Chicken with Tarragon Sauce **54**
Olive-Stuffed Chicken with Almonds **50**
Chicken Breasts with Poblano Chile Strips and Cream **55**
Chicken Cutlets with Fried Capers, Parsley, and Lemon **55**
Cilantro Chicken Patties **59**

THIGHS • LEGS • WINGS
Maple-Glazed Chicken Thighs **58**
Soy Balsamic Chicken Thighs **58**
Hoisin Five-Spice Chicken Legs **59**
Roasted Curry Drumsticks with Yogurt Cumin Sauce **57**
Deep-Fried Chicken Wings with Teriyaki Dipping Sauce **53**

TURKEY
Turkey Burgers with Boursin **60**
Turkey Cutlets with Sautéed Fennel and Carrots **60**

48

Poultry

When in doubt, there's always chicken. Week after week, we toss a bird or two into our shopping cart for easy "automatic pilot" dishes. Unfortunately, as everyone knows too well, repeat performances get boring *fast*. So here are a host of exciting alternatives, like sautéed chicken breasts with spinach, prosciutto, and mozzarella; deep-fried wings with teriyaki sauce; and a whole roasted chicken with olives, oranges, and thyme. When you feel like something spicy, there are curry drumsticks with yogurt cumin sauce. And be sure to give our burgers a try. The turkey burgers with Boursin (on super-size English muffins) are as *Gourmet* as they come.

49

Mustard Roasted Chicken

SERVES 4
Active time: 20 min   Start to finish: 1½ hr

1 (3½- to 4-lb) chicken
½ cup coarse-grained mustard plus
    1 tablespoon
½ cup heavy cream
1 tablespoon chopped fresh flat-leaf
    parsley (optional)

Preheat oven to 400°F.

Cut out backbone from chicken with kitchen shears. Pat chicken dry, then spread flat, skin side up, on a cutting board. Cut a ½-inch slit on each side of chicken in center of triangle of skin between thighs and breasts (near drumsticks) with a knife. Tuck drumstick ends through slits, then tuck wing tips under breasts.

Turn chicken over, skin side down, and spread ¼ cup mustard over chicken and sprinkle with ½ teaspoon salt and ¼ teaspoon black pepper. Put chicken, skin side up, in a small roasting pan, then spread with ¼ cup mustard and sprinkle with ½ teaspoon salt and ¼ teaspoon black pepper.

Roast chicken in middle of oven 30 minutes, then add ½ cup water to pan. Continue to roast chicken until cooked through and an instant-read thermometer inserted into the thickest part of the thigh registers 170°F (do not touch bone), about 45 minutes.

Transfer chicken to cleaned board and skim fat from pan juices. Straddle pan across 2 burners over low heat, then whisk cream and remaining tablespoon mustard into pan juices and deglaze pan by simmering over moderately high heat, stirring and scraping up any brown bits, about 2 minutes. Transfer sauce to a small saucepan and simmer, stirring occasionally, until slightly thickened, about 10 minutes. Stir in parsley and any juices accumulated on board.

Cut chicken into serving pieces and serve with sauce.

Olive-Stuffed Chicken with Almonds

SERVES 4
Active time: 35 min   Start to finish: 35 min

4 boneless chicken breast halves with skin
    (2¼ lb total)
1 cup brine-cured green olives such as
    picholine, pitted and chopped
2 tablespoons unsalted butter
¼ cup whole almonds with skins
2 tablespoons chopped fresh
    flat-leaf parsley

Pat chicken breasts dry, then cut a 2-inch-long horizontal slit in thickest part of each. Stuff each chicken breast with 1½ teaspoons olives, then season with salt and black pepper.

Heat 1 tablespoon butter in a 12-inch nonstick skillet over moderate heat until foam subsides, then toast almonds, stirring frequently, until a few shades darker, 5 to 8 minutes. Transfer with a slotted spoon to a cutting board to cool (do not clean skillet).

Heat skillet over moderately high heat, then add chicken breasts, skin sides down, and sprinkle with remaining olives. Sauté chicken breasts until skins are golden brown, 8 to 10 minutes. Turn chicken breasts over and cook, covered, over moderate heat until just cooked through, 5 to 7 minutes more, then transfer with tongs to plates.

While chicken is cooking, chop almonds.

Add remaining tablespoon butter and 3 tablespoons water to skillet and heat, stirring, until butter is melted. Stir in almonds, parsley, and black pepper to taste. Spoon sauce over chicken.

Roast Cornish Hens with Garlic-Sherry Vinegar Jus

SERVES 2 TO 4
Active time: 20 min   Start to finish: 50 min

2 (1¼-lb) Cornish game hens, gizzards discarded and necks trimmed flush with bodies
1 whole head garlic, left unpeeled and halved crosswise
3 tablespoons unsalted butter, 2 tablespoons of it softened and remaining tablespoon chilled
3 tablespoons Sherry vinegar

Preheat oven to 475°F.

Rinse birds inside and out and pat dry, then rub half of garlic head all over birds. Beginning at neck end of each bird, slide fingers between meat and skin to loosen skin from breast (be careful not to tear skin), then spread ½ tablespoon softened butter under breast skin of each bird, massaging skin from outside to spread butter evenly. Rub birds all over with remaining tablespoon softened butter and season inside and out with salt and black pepper. Arrange, breast sides up, in a buttered flameproof roasting pan just large enough to hold them without crowding (birds are not trussed). Drizzle birds with 1 tablespoon vinegar and put halves of garlic head, cut sides down, in pan.

Roast birds in middle of oven until an instant-read thermometer inserted in thickest part of a thigh (do not touch bone) registers 170°F, about 30 minutes. Transfer birds to a platter and loosely cover with foil to keep warm, then transfer garlic with a spatula to a cutting board.

Press down on softened garlic with spatula to remove cloves from skins, then discard skins. Add garlic, ½ cup water, and remaining 2 tablespoons vinegar to roasting pan. Straddle pan over 2 burners and deglaze pan by simmering over moderately high heat, stirring to incorporate garlic and scraping up brown bits, 2 minutes. Add 1 tablespoon chilled butter and swirl pan to incorporate. Pour sauce through a coarse sieve into a large measuring cup, pressing hard on solids. If sauce measures more than ½ cup, boil in a small saucepan to reduce to ½ cup. Season sauce with salt and black pepper.

If serving 4, halve birds through breast bone and back bone with a large knife. Serve with sauce.

Deep-Fried Chicken Wings with Teriyaki Dipping Sauce

SERVES 4 TO 6 (LIGHT LUNCH)
Active time: 40 min   Start to finish: 40 min

- ½ **cup bottled teriyaki sauce**
- 2 **tablespoons *mirin* (Japanese sweet rice wine)**
- 2 **small scallions, thinly sliced**
- 2 **qt vegetable oil**
- 2 **lb chicken wings (10 to 12)**

Special equipment: a deep-fat thermometer

Stir together teriyaki sauce, *mirin*, and scallions in a bowl.

Heat enough oil to measure 2 inches in a 4- to 5-quart deep heavy pot (preferably cast-iron) over moderately high heat until it registers 360°F on thermometer.

While oil is heating, cut each chicken wing at joints into three pieces with kitchen shears and discard wing tips. Pat wings dry. Just before frying, salt and pepper about 6 pieces, then fry, turning occasionally, until just cooked through, about 6 minutes. Transfer wings with a slotted spoon to paper towels to drain. Season and fry remaining wings in same manner, returning oil to 360°F between batches. Serve with dipping sauce.

Whole Roasted Chicken with Olives, Orange, and Thyme

SERVES 4
Active time: 20 min   Start to finish: 1¼ hr

- 2 **juice oranges**
- 1 **bunch fresh thyme**
- ⅓ **cup Kalamata or other brine-cured black olives, pitted and finely chopped**
- 4 **tablespoons unsalted butter, 3 tablespoons of it softened and 1 tablespoon melted**
- 1 **(4-lb) chicken, rinsed and patted dry**

Special equipment: kitchen string

Preheat oven to 425°F.

Finely grate enough zest from 1 orange to measure 2 teaspoons and squeeze 1 tablespoon juice into a bowl. Chop enough thyme to measure 2 teaspoons. Stir together orange juice, zest, chopped thyme, olives, 3 tablespoons softened butter, and ½ teaspoon each salt and pepper.

Put chicken, breast side up, in a small roasting pan and, beginning at neck end, slide fingers between meat and skin to loosen skin from breast at both ends. Loosen skin from drumsticks, beginning at thigh from inside cavity, with a small, sharp knife. Spread two thirds olive butter under breast skin, spreading over each side of breast and massaging skin from outside to spread butter evenly. Divide remaining butter between each drumstick, massaging skin to spread butter in same manner. Season cavity and skin with salt and black pepper. Quarter remaining orange and place inside cavity along with remaining thyme sprigs. Tie drumsticks together with kitchen string and brush chicken with 1 tablespoon melted butter.

Roast chicken in middle of oven, basting occasionally, until an instant-read thermometer inserted in fleshy part of a thigh registers 170°F, about 1 hour.

Escallopes of Chicken with Tarragon Sauce

SERVES 4
Active time: 15 min   Start to finish: 15 min

- **4 (6-oz) boneless skinless chicken breast halves**
- **4 tablespoons unsalted butter, cut into tablespoon pieces**
- **¼ cup all-purpose flour**
- **½ cup dry white Vermouth**
- **3 tablespoons chopped fresh tarragon**

Remove tenders from chicken and reserve for another use. Pound breasts to a ¼-inch thickness between 2 sheets of plastic wrap with a meat pounder or rolling pin, then season with salt and pepper. Heat 1 tablespoon butter in a 12-inch heavy skillet over moderately high heat until hot but not smoking. Quickly dredge 2 chicken breasts in flour, shaking off excess, then sauté until cooked through, about 3 minutes on each side. Transfer to a platter with tongs and keep warm, loosely covered with foil. Dredge and sauté remaining chicken in 1 tablespoon butter and transfer to platter. Cool skillet 1 minute.

Add Vermouth to skillet and deglaze by simmering over moderately high heat, stirring and scraping up brown bits, 1 minute. Remove from heat and whisk in remaining 2 tablespoons butter 1 piece at a time. Season with salt and black pepper, then stir in tarragon and spoon sauce over chicken.

Chicken Breasts with Spinach, Prosciutto, and Mozzarella

SERVES 4
Active time: 10 min   Start to finish: 25 min

- **4 boneless skinless chicken breast halves (1½ lb total)**
- **1 tablespoon unsalted butter**
- **1 oz fresh baby spinach or basil (1 cup)**
- **4 thin slices prosciutto (3 oz)**
- **4 thin slices fresh mozzarella (⅓ lb)**

Pat chicken dry and season with black pepper. Heat butter in a 12-inch heavy skillet over moderately high heat until hot but not smoking, then sauté chicken, turning once, until golden, about 6 minutes per side. Put ¼ cup spinach, 1 prosciutto slice, and 1 mozzarella slice on top of each breast and cook over moderately low heat, covered, until cheese melts and chicken is cooked through, about 3 minutes.

to flatten meat

A paillard (pie-YAHR), named for a 19th century Parisian chef, is a well-flattened piece of meat—usually veal, beef, or chicken—that is sautéed or grilled. Our favorite meat pounder is brass but you can also find them in stainless steel. The word *pounder* is a bit misleading. The goal is to *stretch*, not mash, the meat to a uniform thickness so that it cooks more quickly and evenly. Bring the pounder straight down onto the meat (between sheets of plastic wrap), then, all in one motion, slide it from the center out to the edge. Repeat in all directions until the entire slice has been flattened. You don't really need a metal meat pounder for the task—a flat side of a wooden meat pounder or a rolling pin will work fine—but a heavier pounder gives you more power. —JANE DANIELS LEAR

Chicken Breasts with Poblano Chile Strips and Cream

SERVES 2
Active time: 40 min   Start to finish: 45 min

½ lb fresh *poblano* chiles (2 to 3)
2 boneless chicken breast halves
    (1½ lb total), with or without skin
1½ tablespoons olive oil
1 medium white onion, halved lengthwise
    and sliced lengthwise ¼-inch thick
¼ cup crème fraîche or sour cream

Lay chiles on their sides on racks of gas burners, then turn flames on moderately high. Roast chiles, turning with tongs, until skins are blistered, 4 to 6 minutes. (Or broil chiles on rack of a broiler pan about 2 inches from heat, turning them, 8 to 10 minutes.) Transfer roasted chiles immediately to a large sealable plastic bag and seal. Steam 10 minutes, then peel or rub off skins and discard stems, seeds, and ribs. Rinse chiles and pat dry, then cut into ¼-inch-thick strips.

Pat chicken dry and season with salt and black pepper. Heat ½ tablespoon oil in a heavy skillet over moderately high heat until hot but not smoking, then sauté chicken, skin or skinned sides down, until golden, 4 to 5 minutes. Turn chicken over and sauté 2 minutes more. Reduce heat to moderately low, then pour off excess fat and cook chicken, covered, until just cooked through, 10 to 15 minutes.

While chicken is cooking, heat remaining tablespoon oil in a 10-inch nonstick skillet over moderate heat, then cook onion, stirring, until softened, 5 to 7 minutes. Add chiles and salt to taste and cook, stirring, 5 minutes. Add crème fraîche and cook, stirring, until just heated through (if using sour cream, do not let boil). Season sauce with salt and black pepper.

Drizzle chicken with any pan juices and serve with sauce.

Chicken Cutlets with Fried Capers, Parsley, and Lemon

SERVES 4
Active time: 15 min   Start to finish: 15 min

¼ cup extra-virgin olive oil
2 tablespoons capers, rinsed, drained,
    and patted dry
1¼ lb chicken cutlets
¼ cup chopped fresh flat-leaf parsley
1½ tablespoons fresh lemon juice, or
    to taste

Heat oil in a 12-inch heavy skillet over moderate heat until hot but not smoking, then fry capers, stirring, until slightly crisp and a shade darker, about 2 minutes. Transfer capers with a slotted spoon to paper towels to drain.

Pat chicken dry and season well with salt and black pepper. Heat oil remaining in skillet over moderately high heat until hot but not smoking, then sauté chicken in batches, turning once, until golden brown, 1 to 1½ minutes per side. Transfer to a platter and keep warm, covered.

Remove skillet from heat. Add parsley and lemon juice to skillet and simmer over moderately high heat, stirring and scraping up any brown bits from bottom of skillet, 1 minute. Pour sauce over chicken and top with fried capers.

Braised Chicken with Shallots, Garlic, and Balsamic Vinegar

SERVES 4
Active time: 40 min   Start to finish: 1¼ hr

- 6 **bacon slices (4 oz), cut crosswise into ¼-inch-wide strips**
- 1 **(3½-lb) chicken, cut into 8 serving pieces**
- 1 **lb shallots, thinly sliced**
- 1 **head garlic, cloves separated and peeled**
- ¼ **cup balsamic vinegar**

Accompaniment: mashed potatoes

Cook bacon in a deep 12-inch heavy skillet over moderately low heat, stirring, until crisp, about 8 minutes. Transfer with a slotted spoon to paper towels to drain and reserve fat in skillet.

While bacon is cooking, pat chicken dry and season with salt and black pepper. Brown, beginning with skin sides down, in 2 batches in fat over moderately high heat, turning, about 8 minutes. Transfer chicken with tongs to a plate and pour off all but 2 tablespoons fat from skillet.

Add sliced shallots to skillet and cook over moderately low heat, covered, stirring occasionally, until softened and pale golden, about 10 minutes. Remove lid and cook shallots, stirring, until deep golden, about 10 minutes more. Add garlic and 1 cup water to skillet and boil, stirring, 1 minute.

Return chicken to skillet, turning pieces to coat, and arrange skin sides up. Gently simmer, covered, until chicken is cooked through and garlic is tender, about 30 minutes.

Transfer chicken with tongs to a serving dish. Add vinegar to sauce and boil, uncovered, mashing garlic with back of a spoon, until slightly thickened. Season sauce with salt and black pepper and pour over chicken, then sprinkle with bacon.

Roasted Curry Drumsticks with Yogurt Cumin Sauce

SERVES 4
Active time: 15 min   Start to finish: 25 hr

If you like your curry very hot, use red curry paste; otherwise go with green.

- ½ **teaspoon cumin seeds**
- 2 **medium garlic cloves**
- 2 **tablespoons bottled green or red Thai curry paste**
- 1 **cup whole-milk yogurt**
- 8 **chicken drumsticks (2½ lb)**

Toast cumin seeds in a small dry heavy skillet over moderate heat, shaking skillet occasionally, until seeds become fragrant and a shade darker, about 3 minutes. Finely grind seeds in an electric coffee/spice grinder or with a mortar and pestle.

Mash garlic to a paste with ½ teaspoon salt using mortar and pestle (or mince and mash with a large heavy knife), then transfer half of garlic to a large bowl and whisk in curry paste, ½ cup yogurt, and half of cumin. Cut 3 (1-inch) slits (about ½-inch deep) in meaty part of each drumstick with a sharp paring knife, then add to yogurt marinade, rubbing marinade into slits.

Transfer drumsticks and marinade to a large sealable plastic bag, forcing out excess air, and marinate, chilled, 24 hours.

Preheat oven to 450°F.

Transfer drumsticks with any marinade clinging to them to a shallow baking pan large enough to hold drumsticks without crowding, then roast in middle of oven until cooked through and golden, 35 to 40 minutes.

Whisk together remaining ½ cup yogurt, garlic paste, and cumin and serve with drumsticks.

Maple-Glazed Chicken Thighs

SERVES 4
Active time: 15 min   Start to finish: 1½ hr

1 **cup pure maple syrup**
¼ **cup fresh lime juice**
3 **tablespoons soy sauce**
2 **teaspoons minced garlic**
8 **chicken thighs (2¼ lb)**

Simmer maple syrup, lime juice, soy sauce, and garlic, stirring occasionally, until reduced to about 1 cup, about 15 minutes.

Preheat oven to 425°F.

Pat chicken dry and season with salt and black pepper. Arrange chicken on a rack set in a roasting pan and roast in middle of oven 15 minutes. Pour 1 cup water down side of roasting pan and brush chicken with some maple glaze. Roast chicken, basting with maple glaze every 10 minutes (you will not use all the glaze), until cooked through, 30 to 35 minutes more.

Transfer chicken with tongs to a platter and remove rack from roasting pan, then skim fat from pan drippings. Set pan across 2 burners, then add remaining maple glaze and deglaze pan by simmering over moderate heat, stirring and scraping up any brown bits, until slightly thickened, about 7 minutes. Transfer sauce to a bowl and serve with chicken.

Soy Balsamic Chicken Thighs

SERVES 4
Active time: 15 min   Start to finish: 25 hr

¼ **cup soy sauce**
3 **tablespoons balsamic vinegar**
2 **tablespoons sugar**
2 **garlic cloves, minced**
8 **chicken thighs (2¾ lb)**

Stir together soy sauce, vinegar, sugar, garlic, ¼ teaspoon salt, and ¼ teaspoon black pepper until sugar is dissolved, then combine with chicken in a large sealable plastic bag, forcing out excess air. Marinate, chilled, 24 hours.

Preheat oven to 425°F.

Transfer chicken and marinade to a shallow baking pan large enough to hold thighs without crowding, then roast in middle of oven, turning twice, until chicken is cooked through, 35 to 40 minutes. Transfer chicken to a serving dish and skim fat from pan juices. Straddle pan across 2 burners, then add ⅓ cup water and deglaze pan by simmering over moderately high heat, stirring and scraping up brown bits, until reduced to about ¼ cup, about 2 minutes.

Serve sauce spooned over chicken.

Hoisin Five-Spice Chicken Legs

SERVES 4
Active time: 10 min   Start to finish: 40 min

**4 chicken legs, thigh and drumstick
    separated**
½ cup hoisin sauce
1 teaspoon Chinese five-spice powder

Preheat oven to 500°F.

Put chicken in a shallow (1-inch-deep) baking pan lined with foil. Stir together hoisin sauce and five-spice powder and brush liberally all over chicken. Bake in upper third of oven until skin is browned and chicken is cooked through, 25 to 30 minutes.

Cilantro Chicken Patties

SERVES 4
Active time: 10 min   Start to finish: 20 min

**1½ lb ground chicken (white and
     dark meat)**
2 teaspoons finely grated fresh lime zest
3 tablespoons finely chopped scallion
1 large egg yolk, lightly beaten
¼ cup chopped fresh cilantro

Preheat broiler.

Stir together all ingredients with 1 teaspoon salt and ¼ teaspoon black pepper in a large bowl until combined well, then form mixture into 4 (4-inch) patties. Lightly oil broiler pan, then broil patties 4 to 6 inches from heat, turning once, until cooked through, 13 to 15 minutes.

Working with five-spice powder in recipes over the years has provided a particularly rich learning experience for us. We discovered that the number five has fundamental significance in ancient Chinese lore: The universe is made up of wood, earth, water, fire, and metal; and much of Chinese music is based on a pentatonic (five-tone) scale. We also learned that there is neither a set formula for the composition of five-spice powder nor a limit to its number of components. It may contain allspice, anise, chile, cinnamon, cloves, fennel, ginger, licorice root, nutmeg, Sichuan peppercorns, thyme, and white peppercorns. The ingredients used, and their proportions, obviously effect the flavor of the final blend. We like Spice Island's brand—a mixture of cinnamon, fennel, licorice root, anise, ginger, chile, allspice, and cloves. —ZANNE STEWART

Turkey Cutlets with Sautéed Fennel and Carrots

SERVES 4
Active time: 20 min   Start to finish: 30 min

1½ lb turkey cutlets
 3 tablespoons unsalted butter
 1 fennel bulb (1 lb), stalks trimmed flush with bulb (reserving fronds), and bulb cored and cut into matchsticks
 3 medium carrots, cut into matchsticks

Preheat oven to 200°F.

Pound cutlets to a ¼-inch thickness between 2 sheets of plastic wrap with a meat pounder or rolling pin and season with salt and black pepper. Heat 2 tablespoons butter in a 12-inch heavy skillet over moderately high heat until foam subsides, then sauté cutlets in batches without crowding, about 2 minutes on each side. Transfer to a plate and keep warm, covered, in oven.

Heat remaining tablespoon butter in skillet over moderately high heat until foam subsides, then sauté fennel bulb and carrots with salt and black pepper to taste, stirring constantly, 3 minutes. Add ½ cup water and cook, covered, stirring occasionally, until water evaporates and vegetables are golden, about 8 minutes. Chop fennel fronds and stir into vegetables.

Serve cutlets with vegetables.

Turkey Burgers with Boursin

SERVES 4
Active time: 15 min   Start to finish: 25 min

Make sure you use a mix of white and dark turkey meat; it will ensure a nice juicy burger.

1½ lb ground turkey (mixed white and dark meat)
 4 super-size English muffins, split and toasted
 1 (5.2-oz) package of garlic and herb Boursin, softened
 2 cups arugula or watercress, coarse stems removed

Preheat broiler.

Mix together turkey, ½ teaspoon salt, and ¼ teaspoon black pepper with your hands until just combined, then form meat into 4 (5-inch) patties.

Lightly oil broiler pan, then broil patties 4 to 6 inches from heat, turning once, until just cooked through, 3 to 4 minutes on each side.

Spread cut sides of muffins with Boursin and make sandwiches with burgers and arugula.

Fish & Shellfish

One of the great things about cooking fish and shellfish is that usually they can be prepared in no time. Many of the recipes here, like our sautéed salmon with zesty *gremolata* and our creamy oyster pan roast, can be on the table in just 20 minutes. Our elegant bacon and rosemary-wrapped halibut in balsamic reduction is so delicious and impressive looking that no one will believe it took only 25 minutes to make. And since many supermarkets have good seafood departments these days, a special trip to the fishmonger is no longer necessary. So the next time someone asks, "what's for dinner?," why not say tarragon lobster salad…or Asian-style flounder baked in parchment…or steamed clams and chorizo?

Tarragon Lobster Salad

SERVES 4 TO 6
Active time: 1 hr   Start to finish: 2 hr

What separates superior lobster salads from merely good ones is, not surprisingly, the quality of the main ingredient. Lobster bought precooked—even from a reputable fish market—tends to be slightly rubbery. So while cooking your own lobster may be a lot of work, your reward will be supremely tender meat. This lobster salad is wonderful on its own—but on a hot dog bun it becomes a perfect lobster roll.

- **4 (1½-lb) live lobsters**
- **¼ cup finely chopped shallot**
- **3 tablespoons fresh lemon juice**
- **⅓ cup mayonnaise**
- **2 tablespoons finely chopped fresh tarragon**

Accompaniment: hot dog buns (preferably top-split), buttered and grilled or toasted

Plunge 2 live lobsters headfirst into an 8-quart pot of boiling salted water. Loosely cover pot and cook lobsters over moderately high heat 9 minutes from time they enter water, then transfer with tongs to sink to cool. Return water to a boil and cook remaining 2 lobsters in same manner.

While lobsters are cooking, stir together shallot, lemon juice, and ½ teaspoon salt in a large bowl and let stand at room temperature 30 minutes.

When lobsters are cool, remove meat from claws, joints, and tails. Discard tomalley, any roe, and shells (or save for another use, see below). Cut meat into ½-inch pieces. Whisk mayonnaise, tarragon, and ¼ teaspoon black pepper into shallot, then add lobster meat and toss gently to coat.

Cooks' notes:
- Lobsters can be cooked and shelled 1 day ahead and chilled, covered.
- Lobster salad can be made 1 day ahead and chilled, covered.

lobster oil

If using live lobsters to make the lobster tarragon salad, don't throw away the shells. We made lobster oil from the debris and were we glad we did. Having the oil around—it keeps frozen for weeks—is like money in the bank. You can use it in vinaigrettes or in mayonnaise for salads (it makes a really elegant potato salad). We also love it drizzled over poached or grilled fish or mashed potatoes. **To make lobster oil:** Coarsely crush 2 lobster carcasses with a mortar and pestle, then sauté with ½ cup canola oil, a tarragon sprig, and a 4-inch strip of orange zest in a 3-quart pot over moderately high heat until very brightly colored, 5 minutes. Add 3½ more cups canola oil and bring to a simmer. Simmer on low heat 40 minutes. Strain through a cheesecloth-lined sieve. Cool and refrigerate up to 2 weeks or freeze up to 1 month. —JANE DANIELS LEAR

Salt Cod Salad

SERVES 4
Active time: 20 min   Start to finish: 3 days

*Be sure to purchase center-cut salt cod. It makes
a world of difference in terms of texture.*

1 lb center-cut skinless boneless salt cod
⅓ cup fresh lemon juice
¼ cup extra-virgin olive oil
1 cup fresh flat-leaf parsley
⅓ cup Kalamata or other brine-cured
   black olives (2 oz), pitted

Put salt cod in a large bowl and add cold water
to cover by 2 inches. Soak cod, chilled, changing
water 3 times a day, up to 3 days. Drain and
rinse well.

Bring cod and enough water to cover just to a
simmer in a 5-quart saucepan, then remove from
heat. (Cod will just flake; do not boil or it will
become tough.) Drain well.

Whisk together lemon juice, oil, and black
pepper to taste in a bowl. When cod is cool
enough to handle, flake into dressing, then add
parsley and olives and toss to combine. Let stand,
covered, at least 30 minutes at room temperature.

Cooks' notes:
• Brands of salt cod differ in their degree of
  saltiness: A less salty variety may need only
  1 day of soaking, while another could require
  up to 3. To test it, simply taste a small piece
  after 1 day; you want it to be pleasantly salty
  but not overwhelming.
• Salad can be made 2 days ahead and chilled,
  covered. It's even more delicious made ahead
  because the flavors have time to develop.
  Bring to room temperature before serving.

Roasted Red Snapper Fillets with Cherry Tomatoes, Scallion, and Basil

SERVES 4
Active time: 20 min   Start to finish: 1½ hr

½ lb cherry tomatoes (1 pint), halved
3 tablespoons extra-virgin olive oil
6 scallions, thinly sliced diagonally and
   dark green slices reserved
   for garnish
4 (6-oz) red snapper fillets with skin
¼ cup thinly sliced basil leaves

Arrange tomatoes, cut sides up, in oil in a
15- by 10- by 1-inch shallow baking pan. Sprinkle
with ½ teaspoon salt and let stand 1 hour at
room temperature.

Preheat oven to 425°F.

Sprinkle white and pale green scallion slices
over tomatoes and bake in upper third of oven
10 minutes. Remove from oven and push
tomatoes to one side of pan with a spoon. Season
fillets with salt and black pepper, then turn in oil
in baking pan to coat and arrange skin sides down
in pan. Spoon some tomatoes over fillets and
bake in upper third of oven until fillets are just
cooked through, about 10 minutes. Scatter basil
and scallion greens over fish and tomatoes
and serve.

Baked Shrimp
with Marinated
Artichoke Hearts

SERVES 4
Active time: 10 min   Start to finish: 45 min

1 **lb large shrimp (25), shelled
    and deveined**
2 **(6- to 7-oz) jars artichoke hearts
    marinated in olive oil, drained,
    reserving ¼ cup liquid, and quartered**
2 **large garlic cloves, thinly sliced**
¼ **cup extra-virgin olive oil**
2 **tablespoons chopped fresh dill**

Accompaniment: hot crusty bread

Preheat oven to 475°F.

Season shrimp with ¼ teaspoon salt and toss together with artichoke hearts and reserved liquid, garlic, olive oil, 1 tablespoon dill, and salt and black pepper to taste in a 1½-quart shallow baking dish. Marinate shrimp 20 minutes at room temperature, turning once or twice.

Bake, covered tightly with foil, in middle of oven, stirring once halfway through baking, until shrimp are just cooked through, about 15 minutes. Serve hot or at room temperature sprinkled with remaining tablespoon dill.

Scallops with
Bacon and Cream
on Toast

SERVES 4
Active time: 10 min   Start to finish: 20 min

3 **slices bacon (3 oz), chopped**
1 **lb sea scallops, tough muscle removed**
½ **cup chilled heavy cream**
2 **tablespoons chopped fresh chives**
6 **slices firm white sandwich bread,
    toasted, crusts discarded, and
    bread halved diagonally**

Cook bacon in a large skillet over medium heat until browned, about 3 minutes, then transfer with a slotted spoon to paper towels to drain (reserve skillet). Pat scallops dry and season with salt and black pepper.

Heat fat remaining in skillet over high heat until hot but not smoking, then sear scallops, turning once, until cooked through, about 5 minutes total. Transfer to platter and keep warm.

Add heavy cream, 1 tablespoon chives, and ¼ teaspoon salt to skillet and boil until slightly thickened, about 1 minute.

Divide scallops among 4 plates. Pour sauce over scallops and sprinkle with bacon and remaining tablespoon chives. Serve with toast.

Oyster Pan Roast

SERVES 2
Active time: 20 min   Start to finish: 20 min

1 small onion, chopped
1½ tablespoons unsalted butter
½ cup heavy cream
**1 (1-lb) container shucked oysters,
    juices drained and discarded**
**4 slices firm white sandwich bread,
    toasted and halved diagonally**

Cook onion in butter in a heavy 10-inch skillet over moderate heat, stirring occasionally, until golden, 5 to 6 minutes. Stir in cream and black pepper to taste and simmer until sauce is slightly thickened, about 2 minutes. Stir in oysters and simmer just until cooked through (edges will curl), about 2 minutes.

Arrange toast triangles in 2 shallow bowls and spoon oysters and sauce over toasts.

Mussels with Potatoes and Spinach

SERVES 2
Active time: 35 min   Start to finish: 35 min

Cultivated mussels—which are less gritty and don't require the extensive cleaning demanded by other varieties—are now widely available, so preparing them at home doesn't take up valuable time. In fact, to save a few more minutes, you can wash the mussels and spinach and mince the garlic while the potatoes are boiling.

1 lb small red boiling potatoes
2 tablespoons olive oil
1 tablespoon minced garlic
**2 lb mussels (preferably cultivated),
    cleaned and beards removed**
½ lb baby spinach, trimmed

Simmer potatoes in enough salted water to cover by 1 inch until just tender, about 15 minutes. Drain and rinse under cold water until cool enough to handle. Pat dry and cut in half (quarter larger potatoes).

Heat 2 tablespoons oil in a large heavy skillet over moderately high heat until hot but not smoking, then sauté potatoes with salt to taste, turning occasionally, until golden brown, about 10 minutes.

While potatoes are sautéing, cook garlic in remaining tablespoon oil in a 5- to 6-quart pot over moderately high heat, stirring, until fragrant. Stir in mussels and ¼ cup water and cook, covered, until mussels are opened, 3 to 5 minutes. (Discard any unopened ones.)

Add spinach to potatoes, tossing until just wilted. Serve potatoes and spinach with mussels.

Romaine-Wrapped Halibut

SERVES 4

Active time: 25 min   Start to finish: 45 min

Most people don't think of cooking romaine lettuce. But in this dish, the romaine wrapping keeps the fish inside moist and tender by releasing its own moisture and protecting the fillet from the heat of the oven. The sweetness of the lettuce goes well with the flavor of the fish.

- 3 tablespoons unsalted butter, softened
- 1 lemon, halved crosswise
- 2 tablespoons finely chopped shallot
- 10 unblemished large outer romaine leaves (from 2 heads)
- 4 (6-oz) pieces halibut, cod, or other white fish fillet (1¼- to 1½-inches thick)

Preheat oven to 450°F.

Coat inside of a 13- by 9-inch glass or ceramic baking or gratin dish with 1 tablespoon butter. Cut 2 thin slices from each lemon half and squeeze juice from remaining lemon.

Mash together remaining 2 tablespoons butter, 1 teaspoon lemon juice, and shallot and season well with salt and black pepper. Sprinkle baking dish with remaining juice.

Cook lettuce in a large pot of salted boiling water 1 minute. Immediately transfer with tongs to a bowl of ice and cold water to stop cooking. Drain lettuce and cut out ribs, leaving top 1 inch of leaves intact.

Spread out 1 lettuce leaf lengthwise on a work surface. Place another leaf on first leaf, overlapping enough to cover any holes (use 2 extra leaves if necessary). Season 1 piece halibut with salt and black pepper and place crosswise in center of lettuce. Spread top of fish with one fourth of shallot butter. Wrap lettuce over fish to form a packet (don't worry if ends aren't covered by lettuce) and transfer to baking dish. Make 3 more packets in same manner, arranging them close together in baking dish. Top each packet with a lemon slice. Cover packets with a sheet of wax or parchment paper, then tightly cover dish with foil.

Bake in middle of oven until centers of packets are just firm to the touch, 15 to 20 minutes, depending on thickness of fish. Serve with pan juices poured over packets.

Clams and Chorizo with Tomato and Garlic

SERVES 4
Active time: 25 min   Start to finish: 40 min

Serve this dish with French bread to get all the delicious sauce.

2 garlic cloves, minced
¼ lb sweet or hot Spanish chorizo (spicy cured pork sausage), cut into ¼-inch dice (¾ cup)
2 tablespoons extra-virgin olive oil
2 (14-oz) cans stewed tomatoes
4 lb littleneck clams (2 inches in diameter), scrubbed

Cook garlic and Spanish chorizo in oil in a 4- to 6-quart heavy pot over moderate heat, stirring occasionally, until garlic is golden, 1 to 2 minutes. Add tomatoes and bring to a simmer, breaking up any large pieces. Simmer, stirring occasionally until sauce thickens, about 15 minutes.

Stir in clams and cook, covered, over moderately high heat, stirring once, until clams open, 9 to 11 minutes. (Discard any that have not opened after 12 minutes.) Serve immediately.

Sautéed Salmon with Gremolata

SERVES 4
Active time: 10 min   Start to finish: 20 min

¼ cup finely chopped fresh flat-leaf parsley
2 teaspoons finely grated fresh lemon zest
1½ teaspoons minced garlic
4 (6-oz) pieces salmon fillet
1 tablespoon olive oil

Toss together parsley, zest, and garlic.

Pat salmon dry and season with salt and black pepper. Heat oil in a 12-inch nonstick skillet over moderately high heat until hot but not smoking, then sauté salmon, skin sides down, 4 minutes. Turn salmon over and sauté until just cooked through, 4 to 5 minutes more. Serve, skin sides down, sprinkled with gremolata.

Shrimp Gratin with Tomatoes and Feta

SERVES 6
Active time: 15 min   Start to finish: 25 min

2 lb large shrimp, peeled and deveined
3 tablespoons extra-virgin olive oil
3 large garlic cloves, finely chopped
1 (14½-oz) can diced tomatoes
   with juice
5 oz feta cheese, finely crumbled

Preheat oven to 450°F.

Season shrimp with salt and black pepper. Heat 1½ tablespoons oil in a 12-inch heavy skillet over moderately high heat until hot but not smoking, then reduce heat to moderate and cook half of shrimp and half of garlic, stirring, until shrimp are opaque but barely cooked through, about 1 minute. Transfer shrimp to a shallow 1½-quart ceramic or glass baking dish. Cook remaining shrimp and garlic in remaining 1½ tablespoons oil in same manner, transferring to dish.

Add tomatoes with juice to skillet and briskly simmer, stirring and scraping up any brown bits, until liquid is reduced by about one third, about 2 minutes. Pour tomatoes over shrimp and sprinkle with feta. Bake in upper third of oven until cheese is melted and bubbling, 5 to 7 minutes.

Fried Squid with Cilantro

SERVES 4
Active time: 15 min   Start to finish: 25 min

3 tablespoons cornstarch
⅓ cup finely chopped fresh cilantro
1 lb cleaned squid, bodies cut
   into 1-inch rings and tentacles
   left whole
1 qt vegetable oil
   Lime wedges

Special equipment: a deep-fat thermometer

Whisk together cornstarch, 2 tablespoons water, and cilantro, then add squid and toss to coat well.

Heat oil in a heavy 4-quart saucepan over moderately high heat until it registers 375°F on thermometer, then fry squid in batches without crowding, turning them, until golden brown and flesh is opaque, 30 to 45 seconds. Transfer with a slotted spoon to paper towels to drain. (Return oil to 375°F between batches.) Season squid with salt and black pepper and serve with lime wedges.

Fried Shrimp with Horseradish Mayonnaise

SERVES 4
Active time: 30 min   Start to finish: 1¼ hr

- ½ cup mayonnaise
- 2 tablespoons bottled horseradish (not drained)
- 1½ lb large shrimp, shelled, leaving last segment of tail intact, and deveined
- 2 cups all-purpose flour
- 6 cups vegetable oil

Special equipment: a deep-fat thermometer

Whisk together mayonnaise, horseradish, and salt to taste.

Stir together 2 cups water and 1 tablespoon salt until salt is dissolved, then add shrimp and let stand at room temperature 30 minutes. Drain well, then arrange in 1 layer on a platter. Sprinkle evenly with 1 tablespoon black pepper and toss well to coat.

Stir together flour and 2 teaspoons salt in a bowl. Heat oil in a heavy 6-quart pot over high heat until it registers 375°F on thermometer.

While oil is heating, toss one fourth of shrimp in flour, shaking off excess. Fry shrimp, stirring occasionally, until golden and just cooked through, about 2 minutes, then transfer with a slotted spoon to paper towels to drain. Dredge and fry remaining shrimp in same manner.

Serve shrimp with horseradish mayonnaise.

Bacon and Rosemary-Wrapped Halibut with Balsamic Reduction

SERVES 4
Active time: 10 min   Start to finish: 25 min

- 4 (6- to 8-oz) halibut fillets (rectangular shaped or long and thin)
- 8 bacon slices
- 4 sprigs fresh rosemary
- ½ cup balsamic vinegar

Pat halibut dry and season with salt and black pepper.

Cook bacon in a large heavy nonstick skillet over moderate heat, turning occasionally, until most of fat is rendered but bacon is still pliable, about 10 minutes. Transfer to paper towels to drain, reserving fat in skillet.

Wrap each fillet evenly with 2 slices bacon, overlapping edges (ends of fillets will be exposed), and weave a sprig of rosemary through bacon on one side. Pour off all but 2 tablespoons fat from skillet and cook fish, rosemary sides down, over moderate heat, turning once, until bacon is crisp and fish is just cooked through, 8 to 10 minutes. Transfer fish to a heated platter. Add vinegar to skillet and simmer until slightly thickened, about 3 minutes. Season sauce with salt and black pepper and pour over fish.

Asian-Style Flounder Baked in Parchment

SERVES 4
Active time: 10 min   Start to finish: 20 min

2 **tablespoons soy sauce**
2 **tablespoons seasoned rice vinegar**
4 **(5-oz) flounder fillets**
2 **teaspoons grated peeled fresh ginger**
2 **scallions, thinly sliced**

Special equipment: 4 (16- by 12-inch) sheets parchment paper

Preheat oven to 425°F.

Stir together soy sauce and rice vinegar in a small bowl.

With short ends of parchment sheets facing you, place 1 fillet parallel to a short end in the middle of each sheet. Sprinkle each fillet with one fourth of ginger, scallions, and soy mixture, then fold parchment over fillet and crimp to seal packets. Place on a baking sheet and bake in middle of oven until packets are puffed and browned, about 6 to 8 minutes.

Poached Sole in White Wine Sauce

SERVES 4
Active time: 10 min   Start to finish: 1 hr

1 **large shallot, finely chopped**
4 **(6-oz) skinless gray sole fillets**
3 **tablespoons unsalted butter, 2 tablespoons of it cold and cut into bits, remaining tablespoon at room temperature**
¾ **cup dry white wine**
1 **tablespoon all-purpose flour**

Sprinkle half of shallot in bottom of a deep 10-inch skillet. Season fish with salt and black pepper, then roll each fillet, skinned side up, into a cylinder and arrange, seam side down, in skillet. Sprinkle fish with remaining shallot and dot with 2 tablespoons cold butter. Pour wine and 4 cups water over fish, adding more water if necessary to barely cover fillets, then cover fish with buttered wax paper. Simmer fish until just cooked through, 8 to 10 minutes. Remove wax paper and transfer fish with a spatula to heated plates, loosely covering with foil to keep warm. Boil poaching liquid over high heat until reduced to about 1 cup, 25 to 30 minutes.

While liquid is boiling, blend together remaining tablespoon butter and flour with your fingers to form a paste. Whisk paste into reduced liquid and boil until thickened, about 2 minutes. Season sauce with salt and spoon over fish.

Oven-Poached Fish in Olive Oil

SERVES 4
Active time: 15 min   Start to finish: 1½ hr

At his New York City restaurant Babbo, chef Mario Batali poaches fish in olive oil. We love the way the fish tastes, so we've adapted the technique for home use. Poaching fish in oil seems like an unusual cooking method, but it's a little like confit, in which meat is cooked in its own fat. The fillets stay extremely moist without any taste of oil. The lemon slices, which lose their tartness when heated with the oil and salt, infuse the dish with wonderful citrus notes.

- ¼ cup capers (preferably in salt), rinsed
- 2½ lb scrod or halibut fillets
    (1-inch thick)
- 1½ large lemons, thinly sliced crosswise
- ¼ cup fresh flat-leaf parsley
- 2 cups extra-virgin olive oil

Preheat oven to 250°F.

Chop half of capers and pat fish dry. Sprinkle fish with 1½ teaspoons salt and ½ teaspoon black pepper and let stand 10 minutes at room temperature. Arrange half of lemon slices in 1 layer in an 8-inch square glass baking dish and arrange fish in 1 layer over lemon. Top with whole and chopped capers, remaining lemon slices, and 3 tablespoons parsley, then pour oil over fish. Bake in middle of oven, uncovered, until fish just flakes and is cooked through, 1 to 1¼ hours.

Serve fish with some of lemon slices, capers, and oil spooned over. Sprinkle with remaining tablespoon parsley.

Cooks' note:
• Lemon oil can be used again as a vinaigrette, in mashed potatoes, or for cooking. To reuse oil, strain it through a paper-towel-lined sieve, then cool to room temperature. It keeps, covered and chilled, 1 week.

Vegetarian

even die-hard steak lovers occasionally enjoy a break from meat. And rest assured, with vegetarian recipes like these, no one will go hungry. Polenta with sautéed mushrooms; pizza with eggplant, tomato, and smoked mozzarella; mustard greens risotto; and cheese-stuffed ancho chiles with black beans are all stick-to-your-ribs fare. Those looking for something lighter will find that lentil, spinach, and tomato stew; and chickpeas with tomatoes and allspice fit the bill. To keep an eye on time, we used prepared pie dough, frozen pizza dough, and canned beans—all legitimate shortcuts—but vegetables are super fresh. After all, they're the star of the show.

Tomato, Goat Cheese, and Onion Tart

SERVES 4
Active time: 20 min   Start to finish: 35 min

Before you call us on this "6-ingredient recipe," we hasten to point out that the tart is just as delicious without the fresh basil leaf garnish.

1 (9-inch) prepared pie dough, thawed if frozen
3 tablespoons olive oil
1 large onion, very thinly sliced
6 oz crumbled goat cheese (1⅓ cups)
1 lb plum tomatoes, thinly sliced crosswise

Garnish: fresh basil leaves
Special equipment: a 9-inch tart pan with removable bottom; pie weights or raw rice

Preheat oven to 375°F.

If necessary, roll out dough on a lightly floured surface into an 11-inch round and fit into tart pan. Trim excess dough, leaving a ½-inch overhang, then fold overhang inward and press against side of pan to reinforce edge. Lightly prick bottom and sides with a fork.

Line tart shell with foil and fill with pie weights. Bake in middle of oven until pastry is pale golden around rim, about 20 minutes. Carefully remove foil and weights and bake until golden all over, 8 to 10 minutes more. Cool in pan on a rack.

While tart shell is baking, heat 2 tablespoons oil in a 12-inch heavy skillet over moderate heat, then cook onion with salt and black pepper to taste, stirring frequently, until golden brown, 15 to 20 minutes.

Preheat broiler.

Spread onion over bottom of tart shell and top with 1 rounded cup goat cheese. Arrange tomatoes, slightly overlapping, in concentric circles over cheese. Sprinkle with remaining cheese and salt and black pepper to taste and drizzle with remaining tablespoon oil. Put foil over edge of crust to prevent overbrowning.

Put tart pan on a baking sheet and broil tart about 7 inches from heat until cheese starts to brown slightly, 3 to 4 minutes.

Swiss Chard Frittata with Mascarpone

SERVES 6 TO 8
Active time: 15 min   Start to finish: 25 min

7 whole large eggs plus 3 large egg whites
**1 lb Swiss chard, tough stems discarded
    and leaves chopped into 1-inch pieces**
2 teaspoons extra-virgin olive oil
2 medium garlic cloves, minced
½ cup mascarpone cheese

Preheat broiler.

Whisk together whole eggs and whites with ¼ teaspoon salt and ¼ teaspoon black pepper in a large bowl.

Cook Swiss chard in oil in an ovenproof 12-inch nonstick skillet over moderate heat, stirring, until tender and any liquid chard gives off is evaporated, about 8 minutes. Add garlic and cook, stirring, 1 minute. Add egg mixture and cook over moderately high heat, lifting up cooked egg around edge to let uncooked egg flow underneath, 3 to 5 minutes (eggs will still be moist). Dollop mascarpone at 2-inch intervals over frittata.

Broil frittata 6 inches from heat until set, puffed, and golden brown, 1 to 2 minutes and cool slightly, about 5 minutes. Loosen edge of frittata, then slide onto a platter and cut into wedges. Serve warm or at room temperature.

Cooks' note:
• If your skillet isn't ovenproof, wrap handle with heavy-duty foil (or a double layer of regular foil) before broiling.

Fennel, Leek, and Potato Gratin

SERVES 4
Active time: 10 min   Start to finish: 1½ hr

As a main course, this dish can be very rich; you can pair it with our Boston lettuce salad with honey mustard and herbs (page 25) for balance.

**2 medium fennel bulbs (sometimes called
    anise; 1½ lb)**
**3 large leeks (white and pale green parts
    only), thinly sliced**
**1½ lb yellow-fleshed potatoes such as
    Yukon Gold, peeled and thinly sliced**
¾ cup heavy cream
1½ oz freshly grated parmesan (½ cup)

Preheat oven to 400°F.

Trim fennel stalks flush with bulb, discarding stalks and thinly slice bulb lengthwise. Wash leeks well in a bowl of cold water, then lift out and drain in a sieve. Toss fennel, leeks, and potatoes with 1 teaspoon salt and ¼ teaspoon black pepper in a large bowl, then spread evenly in a 4-quart baking dish and cover tightly with foil. Bake in middle of oven until tender, 1 hour.

Bring cream to a boil in a small saucepan, then remove from heat. Remove foil from gratin and pour cream evenly over vegetables. Sprinkle with parmesan and bake, uncovered, until bubbling and top is golden, 15 to 20 minutes.

Roasted Butternut Squash and Watercress Salad

SERVES 2
Active time: 20 min   Start to finish: 1 hr

1½ lb butternut squash, halved,
       seeded, and cut diagonally
       into 2-inch-wide wedges
  2 tablespoons plus 1 teaspoon
       extra-virgin olive oil
  ½ cup pecans
  1 bunch watercress, coarse
       stems discarded
  ½ tablespoon Sherry vinegar

Preheat oven to 425°F.

Toss squash with 1 tablespoon oil in a shallow baking pan and roast in middle of oven, turning occasionally, until golden and tender, about 40 minutes. Keep warm, covered.

Heat 1 teaspoon oil in a heavy skillet over moderate heat until hot but not smoking, then toast pecans, stirring, until fragrant and 1 shade darker, about 4 minutes. Transfer nuts with a slotted spoon to paper towels to drain and season with salt and black pepper. Cool completely.

Toss watercress with vinegar, remaining tablespoon oil, pecans, and salt and black pepper to taste in a bowl.

Transfer squash to serving plates and top with salad.

Mushroom Bruschetta

SERVES 6 (LUNCH)
Active time: 10 min   Start to finish: 35 min

  1 lb cremini mushrooms, trimmed
       and quartered
  6 tablespoons extra-virgin olive oil
  2 medium garlic cloves, minced
  6 (½-inch-thick) slices country-style
       bread, each halved crosswise
  8 oz Taleggio or Italian Fontina cheese,
       thinly sliced

Preheat oven to 400°F.

Toss mushrooms with 3 tablespoons oil, garlic, ½ teaspoon salt, and ¼ teaspoon black pepper in a 1½-quart baking dish. Bake in upper third of oven, stirring occasionally, until tender and sizzling, about 25 minutes.

While mushrooms are roasting, arrange bread in 1 layer on a baking sheet and brush tops with remaining 3 tablespoons oil. Toast in middle of oven until golden brown, about 15 minutes.

Arrange 2 or 3 slices of cheese on each toast, then top cheese with ¼ cup mushrooms. Bake bruschetta in upper third of oven until cheese is melted, 3 to 5 minutes. Season with black pepper.

Cooks' note:
• Taleggio and Fontina, both soft cheeses, are easier to slice if partially frozen. Freeze 30 minutes before slicing.

Fried Eggs and Asparagus with Parmesan

SERVES 2 (MAIN COURSE)
Active time: 20 min   Start to finish: 25 min

This simple but compelling supper dish is based on Marcella Hazan's recipe for gratinéed asparagus with fried eggs in Essentials of Classic Italian Cooking. *Hot from the oven, yolks and spears and cheese coalesce into buttery magic.*

1½ **lb medium asparagus, trimmed and, if desired, peeled**
2½ **tablespoons unsalted butter**
⅔ **cup freshly grated Parmigiano-Reggiano (2 oz)**
4 **large eggs**

Special equipment: 2 (9½-inch) oval ovenproof gratin dishes (about 1½ inches deep)

Preheat oven to 425°F.

Cook asparagus in a large deep skillet of boiling salted water until crisp-tender, about 4 minutes. Transfer with tongs to paper towels to drain.

Generously butter both gratin dishes using ½ tablespoon butter total, then divide asparagus between them. Season with salt and black pepper, then sprinkle with half of cheese.

Heat remaining 2 tablespoons butter in a 10-inch nonstick skillet over moderately high heat until foam subsides, then fry eggs, seasoning with salt and black pepper, until whites are barely set, about 2 minutes. Carefully transfer 2 eggs to each gratin dish with a slotted spatula, placing on top of asparagus. Sprinkle eggs with remaining cheese and drizzle with any butter remaining in skillet.

Bake in upper third of oven until cheese is melted and eggs are cooked as desired, 4 to 5 minutes for runny yolks.

Cooks' note:
• If eggs are served with runny yolks, they will not be fully cooked, which may be of concern if there is a problem with salmonella in your area.

Escarole and Beans

SERVES 4
Active time: 15 min   Start to finish: 25 min

- 3 tablespoons olive oil
- 1 large onion, chopped
- 2 large carrots, cut into ½-inch pieces
- 2½ lb escarole, coarsely chopped
- 1 (19-oz) can *cannellini* beans, rinsed
     and drained

Heat 2 tablespoons oil in 6-quart saucepan, over moderately high heat, then sauté onion and carrots, stirring occasionally, until golden, about 7 minutes. Add escarole, tossing to coat with oil, and cook 1 minute. Add ½ cup water and simmer over moderate heat, covered, until carrots and escarole are tender, about 10 minutes. Stir in beans and salt and black pepper to taste and remove from heat. Transfer to a serving bowl and drizzle with remaining tablespoon oil.

Pan-Fried Tofu and Bok Choy

SERVES 4
Active time: 10 min   Start to finish: 25 min

- 1 lb extra-firm tofu, drained and cut
     crosswise into 6 equal slices
- 2 tablespoons vegetable oil
- 2 lb bok choy, trimmed and cut crosswise
     into 1-inch-thick slices
- 3 tablespoons teriyaki sauce

Pat tofu dry between several layers of paper towels, pressing lightly. Repeat drying process 3 times, then season with salt and black pepper.

Heat oil in a 12-inch heavy skillet over moderately high heat until hot but not smoking, then cook tofu until golden brown on both sides, about 6 minutes total, and transfer with a spatula to paper towels to drain. Add bok choy to skillet and cook over moderately high heat, covered, stirring occasionally, until tender, about 6 minutes. Remove from heat and stir in teriyaki sauce. Halve tofu slices diagonally and serve over bok choy.

tofu

We've all found ourselves staring meditatively at the snowy blocks of tofu, or soybean curd, in the produce section of the grocery store. We know the stuff is good for you, but then again, it doesn't really draw a body in. You need to look at its innocuousness, though, as an opportunity, for it soaks up the flavor of a sauce or marinade like a sponge (case in point—our pan-fried tofu and bok choy above). Because tofu is fragile, choose the texture according to what you're cooking: Buy extra-firm or firm for frying, soft for stir-frying or braising, and silken for soups or steaming. Tofu keeps, in a container of water, three or four days in the refrigerator. (Change the water every day.) —JANE DANIELS LEAR

Warm Lentil, Spinach, and Tomato Stew

SERVES 4
Active time: 20 min   Start to finish: 30 min

- 1   cup French green lentils (7 oz), picked over
- 4   cups grape tomatoes (1¼ lb), halved
- 2   teaspoons tarragon vinegar
- 6   tablespoons olive oil
- ¼   lb baby spinach (5 cups packed)

Bring lentils and 3 cups cold water to a boil in a 3-quart saucepan, then simmer, partially covered, until tender, about 25 minutes.

While lentils are cooking, purée 2 cups tomatoes, tarragon vinegar, 1 tablespoon water, ¾ teaspoon salt, and ¼ teaspoon black pepper in a blender. With motor running, add 4 tablespoons oil in a slow stream and blend until emulsified.

Heat remaining 2 tablespoons oil in a 12-inch nonstick skillet over moderately high heat until hot but not smoking, then cook remaining 2 cups tomatoes until they begin to "melt," about 3 minutes. Add spinach a handful at a time and cook until wilted, about 2 minutes, then remove from heat.

Drain lentils in a sieve, then transfer to a bowl and season with salt. Add dressing, spinach, and tomatoes and toss gently to combine.

Cheese-Stuffed Ancho Chiles with Black Beans

SERVES 4
Active time: 20 min   Start to finish: 4 hr

- 8   medium to large whole dried *ancho* chiles (4 oz total)
- 1   (14- to 15-oz) can stewed tomatoes
- 2   (19-oz) cans black beans, rinsed and drained
- ⅓   cup chopped fresh cilantro
- ¾   lb Monterey Jack cheese, coarsely grated (4 cups)

Soak chiles in cold water to cover in a large bowl, gently turning chiles occasionally, until well softened, at least 3 hours (they will turn a brighter red).

Preheat oven to 350°F.

Stir together tomatoes (with juice), beans, half of cilantro, and salt and black pepper to taste in a 3-quart shallow baking dish.

Drain chiles, then carefully slit each lengthwise with your fingers and discard seeds and any large ribs, leaving flesh and stems intact. Rinse gently and pat dry. Stuff chiles with cheese, leaving slightly open to expose cheese, and arrange, cut sides up, in 1 layer on top of bean mixture. Season with salt and cover with foil, then bake in middle of oven until beans are bubbling and cheese is melted, about 30 minutes. Remove foil and bake 5 minutes more.

Sprinkle remaining cilantro over chiles.

Cooks' note:
• Chiles can soak up to 8 hours at room temperature.

Ricotta Gnocchi with Roasted Tomato

SERVES 4

Active time: 35 min   Start to finish: 1¼ hr

A sprinkling of Parmigiano-Reggiano and fresh basil can be a nice addition to this dish.

- **2   lb plum tomatoes, trimmed and halved lengthwise**
- **½   stick (¼ cup) unsalted butter**
- **3   large eggs**
- **1   (15-oz) container ricotta, preferably fresh**
- **1   cup all-purpose flour**

Roast tomatoes:

Preheat oven to 400°F.

Put tomatoes, cut sides up, in 1 layer in a 13- by 9-inch baking dish. Dot with 2 tablespoons butter and season well with salt and black pepper. Roast in middle of oven until skins are wrinkled and beginning to brown, about 45 minutes. Cool in baking dish.

Make gnocchi while tomatoes roast:

Bring a large pot of salted water to a boil.

Beat together eggs and ricotta in a large bowl with an electric mixer, then stir in flour, 1 teaspoon kosher salt, and ½ teaspoon black pepper. (Batter will be soft.)

Use 2 teaspoons (flatware, not measuring spoons) to form gnocchi: Scoop up a rounded teaspoon of batter, then use second spoon to scoop mixture off spoon and into boiling water. Make 9 more gnocchi in same manner.

Simmer briskly until gnocchi are just firm in center and cooked through, about 5 minutes. Transfer with a slotted spoon to a platter and cool, covered with damp paper towels. Continue making gnocchi in batches of 10.

Make sauce and sauté gnocchi:

When tomatoes are cool enough to handle, peel and seed over roasting pan. Slice tomato flesh lengthwise ¼-inch thick and put in a saucepan. Scrape skins, seeds, and any juices from roasting pan into a fine sieve set over saucepan with tomatoes and press on solids to extract juices. Discard skins and seeds.

Stir ¼ cup water into tomatoes and bring to a low simmer over low heat. While tomatoes are coming to a simmer, melt remaining 2 tablespoons butter in a 12-inch nonstick skillet over moderate heat, then cook gnocchi, turning gently, until heated through, 4 to 5 minutes.

Season gnocchi with salt and black pepper and serve with warm tomatoes.

Mustard Greens Risotto

SERVES 4
Active time: 30 min   Start to finish: 45 min

3 cups vegetable broth
**1 lb mustard greens, stems and
center ribs discarded**
1 large onion, chopped
3 tablespoons unsalted butter
1½ cups Arborio rice

Bring broth, 4 cups water, and ½ teaspoon salt
to a boil in a 3- to 4-quart saucepan. Add mustard
greens in batches and simmer, stirring
occasionally, until tender, 8 to 10 minutes.
Transfer greens with tongs to a large sieve set
over a bowl to drain, gently pressing on greens
to extract more liquid. Add liquid in bowl to
simmering broth and keep at a bare simmer,
covered. Chop cooked mustard greens.

Cook onion in 2 tablespoons butter in a 4-quart
heavy saucepan over moderate heat, covered,
stirring occasionally, until golden, about
5 minutes. Add rice and cook, stirring, 1 minute.
Add ½ cup simmering broth and cook at a strong
simmer, stirring constantly, until broth is
absorbed. Continue simmering rice and adding
broth, about ½ cup at a time, stirring constantly
and letting each addition be absorbed before
adding next, until rice is creamy-looking but
still al dente, 17 to 18 minutes total (it should be
the consistency of thick soup). (There will be
leftover broth).

Add mustard greens and remaining tablespoon
butter and cook, stirring, until heated through and
butter is melted, about 1 minute. Season risotto
with salt and black pepper and, if desired, thin
with some remaining broth.

Polenta with Sautéed Mushrooms

SERVES 4
Active time: 35 min   Start to finish: 45 min

1 cup yellow cornmeal
½ stick (¼ cup) unsalted butter
**¾ cup freshly grated Parmigiano-
Reggiano**
1½ lb mushrooms, thinly sliced
3 garlic cloves, finely chopped

Whisk together cornmeal, 1 teaspoon salt, and
4½ cups cold water in a 4-quart saucepan. Bring
to a boil over high heat, whisking frequently, then
reduce heat to moderately low and cook, stirring
frequently, until very thick, 25 to 30 minutes. Stir
in 2 tablespoons butter and ½ cup cheese.

Heat remaining 2 tablespoons butter in a
12-inch heavy skillet over moderately high heat
until foam subsides, then sauté mushrooms
and garlic, stirring frequently, until any liquid
mushrooms give off is evaporated and mushrooms
are golden, 10 to 12 minutes. Season with salt
and black pepper. Top polenta with mushrooms
and sprinkle with remaining ¼ cup cheese.
Serve immediately.

Chickpeas with Tomatoes and Allspice

SERVES 4
Active time: 35 min   Start to finish: 45 min

2 (15- to 19-oz) cans chickpeas,
   rinsed and drained
1 (14½-oz) can stewed tomatoes
   Rounded ¼ teaspoon ground allspice
2 tablespoons chopped fresh
   flat-leaf parsley
1 cup crumbled feta (5 oz)

Slip off skins from chickpeas and discard skins. Simmer chickpeas, stewed tomatoes, ⅓ cup water, allspice, and 1 tablespoon parsley in a 2- to 3-quart saucepan over moderate heat, stirring occasionally, 10 minutes. Remove from heat and stir in feta, remaining tablespoon parsley, and black pepper to taste.

Moist, crumbly feta isn't a complex cheese, but a recent tasting revealed surprising differences in flavor and texture. Most of the ones we tried were generic—from retailers who buy the cheese in bulk from various importers and package it themselves. According to cheese authority Steve Jenkins, Greek feta is nowadays made in Sardinia (because the worldwide demand is so huge) and sent to Greece, where it is shipped around the world. Our favorites were imported from Boboris (sharp and salty but balanced) and Mt. Vikos (a piquant blend of sheep and goat's milk). If you find yourself in Greece, though, look for artisanal barrel-aged feta; the producers are a vanishing breed. The best Bulgarian fetas—all no-name, bulk sheep's-milk cheeses—were tangy rather than sharp, and very rich. And about five years ago, when France restricted the gathering of sheep's milk for Roquefort production (one way to keep demand for the cheese high) many producers there decided to use the resulting surplus for export-market feta. Valbresco brand has a lovely herbaceous quality that takes you straight to the French countryside. And Israel's feta—mild yet full of character—is great for breakfast. The French and Israeli fetas were smooth and very creamy compared to the others. —JANE DANIELS LEAR

feta

Pizza with Eggplant, Tomato, and Smoked Mozzarella

SERVES 2
Active time: 30 min   Start to finish: 50 min

For easier handling, be sure to dust your hands with flour before working with the pizza dough.

- **1 lb eggplant, peeled if desired and cut crosswise into 12 (½-inch-thick) slices**
- **2 tablespoons olive oil**
- **1 lb fresh or thawed frozen pizza dough (store-bought)**
- **½ lb coarsely shredded smoked mozzarella (2 cups)**
- **2 medium tomatoes, cored and cut crosswise into 12 (¼-inch-thick) slices**

Special equipment: 2 large heavy baking sheets

Preheat oven to 400°F.

Brush both sides of eggplant slices with oil and arrange in 1 layer in an oiled shallow baking pan. Roast in middle of oven until tender, about 15 minutes, then cool. Leave oven on.

Dust hands with flour. Form half of dough into a 10-inch round by holding 1 edge of dough in the air with both hands and letting bottom edge touch work surface, then move hands around edge (like turning a steering wheel), allowing weight of dough to stretch round to a rough 8-inch circle. Flour your fists and with them stretch dough from center of underside, turning dough to maintain a circle, until about 10 inches in diameter. Put round on a floured heavy baking sheet. Make a second round in same manner and put on other floured heavy baking sheet.

Increase oven heat to 500°F and set oven rack in lowest position.

Sprinkle ½ cup cheese on each dough round, then arrange half of eggplant and tomato slices on each round, leaving a 1-inch border. Season vegetables with salt and black pepper and sprinkle evenly with remaining cup cheese.

Bake pizzas 1 at a time on lowest rack in oven until underside of crust is browned and cheese is bubbling, 12 to 15 minutes.

Cooks' note:
- If you have a pizza stone, heat it on oven floor (for an electric oven, place on lowest rack) 1 hour at 500°F. Make 1 pizza at a time, assembling it on a well-floured peel or baking sheet and sliding it onto stone. Bake each pizza 7 to 8 minutes.

BEEF

Blue Cheese Hamburgers with Caramelized Onions **94**

Braised Short Ribs with Dijon Mustard **96**

Oven-Braised Beef with Tomato Sauce and Garlic **94**

Rib-Eye Steak au Poivre with Balsamic Reduction **92**

Sautéed Filet Mignon with Olives and Capers **93**

Stir-Fried Beef with Cilantro **93**

PORK

Cider-Braised Pork Shoulder with Caramelized Onions **99**

Currant Mustard-Glazed Ham **100**

Kielbasa with Sauerkraut, Mushrooms, and Onions **100**

Grilled Pork Tenderloin with Mojo Sauce **97**

Pork Chops with Apples and Cream **97**

LAMB

Braised Lamb with Honey and Garlic **101**

Lamb Chops with Coarse-Grain Mustard **101**

VEAL

Pounded Veal Chop with Arugula Salad **102**

Veal Paprikas **102**

Weiner Schnitzel with Spaetzle **103**

Meats

around the world with only five ingredients? Our cooks love a challenge, and they stepped up to the plate with these meat dishes. A South American inspired pork tenderloin with a hefty dose of *mojo* sauce will have your tastebuds doing the tango. Hungary? A hearty Hungarian veal paprikas is sure to satiate you, and Austrian weiner schnitzel and homemade spaetzle will become a few of your favorite things. Poland inspired a one-dish wonder of kielbasa with sauerkraut, mushrooms, and onions. We also added some familiar backyard regulars like hamburgers stuffed with blue cheese and topped with caramelized onions as well as a pounded veal chop with arugula salad. After all, there's no place like home.

Rib-Eye Steak au Poivre with Balsamic Reduction

SERVES 4
Active time: 10 min   Start to finish: 30 min

- **2 tablespoons whole black peppercorns**
- **4 (¾-inch-thick) boneless rib-eye steaks (¾ lb each)**
- **1 tablespoon vegetable oil**
- **2 tablespoons unsalted butter**
- **½ cup balsamic vinegar**

Accompaniment: crisp rosemary potatoes (page 120)
Special equipment: a mortar and pestle

Coarsely grind peppercorns with mortar and pestle. Pat steaks dry and coat both sides with peppercorns, pressing to adhere. Season with salt.

Heat oil with 1 tablespoon butter in a 12-inch heavy skillet over moderately high heat until hot but not smoking. Reduce heat to moderate and cook steaks, 2 at a time, about 4 minutes on each side for medium-rare. Transfer steaks to a platter.

Add vinegar to skillet and deglaze by boiling over high heat, stirring and scraping up brown bits, then simmer until reduced to about ¼ cup. Remove from heat and whisk in remaining tablespoon butter until melted. Season sauce with salt and drizzle over steaks.

Sautéed Filet Mignon with Olives and Capers

SERVES 4
Active time: 8 min   Start to finish: 25 min

½ cup Kalamata or other brine-cured
  black olives at room temperature,
  pitted
1 tablespoon bottled capers at room
  temperature, drained
4 (1½-inch-thick) filets mignons
  (2 lb total)
1 tablespoon olive oil

Mince together olives and capers.

Pat steaks dry and season with salt and black pepper. Heat oil in a 10- to 12-inch heavy skillet over high heat until hot but not smoking, then brown steaks, about 3 minutes on each side. Reduce heat to moderate and cook steaks 7 minutes more on each side for medium-rare. Transfer to plates and let stand 5 minutes.

Serve steaks topped with olives and capers.

Stir-Fried Beef with Cilantro

SERVES 4
Active time: 15 min   Start to finish: 15 min

1 tablespoon Asian chile paste
2 tablespoons vegetable oil
1 lb boneless sirloin, cut into
  ¼-inch-thick slices
¼ cup chopped fresh cilantro plus
  ½ cup fresh cilantro leaves
1 teaspoon *naam pla* (Asian fish sauce)

Stir together chile paste and ⅓ cup water.

Heat a wok or 12-inch heavy skillet over high heat until a bead of water dropped on cooking surface evaporates immediately. Add 1 tablespoon oil and heat until just smoking, then stir-fry half of beef until browned, about 30 seconds, and transfer to a bowl. Add remaining oil to wok and stir-fry remaining beef in same manner. Return all beef and any juices accumulated in bowl to wok and stir-fry 30 seconds more. Add chile-paste water and ¼ cup chopped cilantro and stir-fry until liquid is reduced to about ¼ cup, about 1 minute. Remove skillet from heat and stir in *naam pla* and salt to taste.

Serve sprinkled with cilantro leaves.

Blue Cheese Hamburgers with Caramelized Onions

SERVES 4
Active time: 15 min   Start to finish: 15 min

1½ lb ground sirloin beef
3 oz mild blue cheese such as Saga,
     crumbled (8 tablespoons)
2 tablespoons olive oil
1 large onion, thinly sliced
4 hamburger buns

Quarter beef and form into 4 balls, then make a large indentation in center of each ball with your thumb. Quarter cheese and form into 4 balls, then put 1 ball into each indentation. Shape beef over cheese to enclose and flatten each burger to ¾-inch thick (about 4 inches wide).

Heat oil in a 12-inch heavy skillet over moderately high heat until hot but not smoking, then reduce heat to moderate and cook onion, stirring frequently, until softened and golden, 10 to 12 minutes. Transfer to a bowl and season with salt and black pepper to taste.

Season burgers with salt and black pepper. Heat cleaned skillet over high heat until hot but not smoking, then reduce heat to moderate and cook burgers, turning once, about 5 minutes on each side for medium-rare.

Serve burgers on buns topped with onion.

Oven-Braised Beef with Tomato Sauce and Garlic

SERVES 6
Active time: 15 min   Start to finish: 4¼ hr

*This recipe was inspired by Aunt Gladys's beef, from Laurie Colwin (*Gourmet, *January 1992), and Nathalie Waag's leg of lamb with tomatoes and garlic (*Gourmet, *September 1986). Leftovers have many possibilities: The meat can be served hot in thick, melting chunks, carved up cold for sandwiches, or cubed for salads.*

1 (28-oz) can whole tomatoes,
     including juice
1 (3- to 3½-lb) boneless chuck roast
1 head garlic, separated into cloves
     (unpeeled)

Accompaniment: orzo

Preheat oven to 300°F.

Coarsely chop tomatoes with juice in a food processor. Put roast in an ovenproof 4- to 5-quart heavy pot or a casserole dish with a lid. Pour tomatoes over roast and scatter garlic around it, then season with salt and black pepper. Braise roast in middle of oven, covered, until very tender, 3 to 4 hours.

Cut roast into ¼-inch-thick slices and serve with sauce and garlic.

Cooks' note:
• The best chuck roasts for this recipe come from the supermarket—fancy butcher shops' meat is too lean and often becomes dry when cooked.

Braised Short Ribs with Dijon Mustard

SERVES 4
Active time: 45 min   Start to finish: 3 hr

This dish was inspired by Daniel Boulud's Café Boulud Cookbook, *in which the chef begins by reducing a great deal of red wine. This technique produces a rich and delicious sauce that tastes as if many days—and ingredients—were required.*

- 4 **cups dry red wine**
- 4 **lb beef short ribs (also called flanken)**
- 10 **shallots (10 oz), trimmed and halved if large**
- 3 **tablespoons coarse-grain Dijon mustard plus additional to taste**
- 6 **plum tomatoes, halved lengthwise**

Boil wine in a 2-quart heavy saucepan until reduced to about 1 cup.

While wine is reducing, pat ribs dry and cut crosswise into 1-rib pieces (each about 2½ inches long). Season well with salt and black pepper.

Heat a dry 5-quart heavy pot over moderately high heat until hot, then brown ribs well in 3 batches, about 8 minutes for each batch. Transfer with tongs to a bowl.

Reduce heat to moderate and brown shallots well in fat remaining in pot, stirring. Transfer with a slotted spoon to another bowl.

Stir wine and mustard into juices in pot. Add ribs and simmer, covered, 1¾ hours. Gently stir in shallots and tomatoes and continue to simmer, covered, without stirring, until meat is very tender, about 40 minutes more.

Carefully transfer ribs, shallots, and tomatoes to a platter and skim off any fat from cooking liquid. Season sauce with salt, black pepper, and additional mustard to taste and pour over ribs.

Pork Chops with Apples and Cream

SERVES 4
Active time: 25 min   Start to finish: 30 min

4   (8-oz) rib pork chops (½-inch thick)
2   tablespoons olive oil
2   apples (preferably Granny Smith)
      peeled, cored, and sliced lengthwise
      ⅓-inch thick
½   cup heavy cream
2   teaspoons cider vinegar

Pat pork chops dry and season with salt and black pepper. Heat oil in a 12-inch heavy skillet over moderately high heat until hot but not smoking, then brown chops, turning once, about 4 minutes on each side, and transfer to a plate.

Cook apples, turning occasionally, until golden and softened, 5 to 7 minutes. Transfer three fourths of apples to a serving platter. Add cream and ½ cup water to skillet and simmer, stirring and scraping up brown bits, until thickened slightly, about 2 minutes. Return chops to skillet and simmer, covered, until cooked through, about 3 minutes. Transfer chops and apples (keeping sauce in skillet) to platter. Stir vinegar into sauce in skillet off heat and season with salt and black pepper. Pour sauce over chops and apples.

Grilled Pork Tenderloin with Mojo Sauce

SERVES 4
Active time: 30 min   Start to finish: 35 min

2   juice oranges
4   garlic cloves, minced
3   tablespoons olive oil
1   teaspoon dried oregano, crumbled
2   (¾-lb) pork tenderloins

Prepare grill for cooking. If using a charcoal grill, open vents on bottom of grill and lid.

Squeeze enough juice from oranges to measure 5 tablespoons. Mash garlic to a paste with ½ teaspoon salt using a mortar and pestle (or mince and mash with a large heavy knife), then whisk together with orange juice, 2 tablespoons oil, and ½ teaspoon oregano.

Pat pork dry and rub each tenderloin with ½ tablespoon oil, ½ teaspoon salt, ¼ teaspoon black pepper, and ¼ teaspoon oregano.

When fire is hot (you can hold your hand 5 inches above rack for 1 to 2 seconds), grill pork on lightly oiled grill rack, covered with lid, turning once, until an instant-read thermometer inserted diagonally into center of each tenderloin registers 155°F, 12 to 14 minutes total. Let pork stand 5 minutes before slicing.

Serve pork drizzled with *mojo* sauce.

Cider-Braised Pork Shoulder with Caramelized Onions

SERVES 4 TO 6
Active time: 30 min   Start to finish: 3 hr

Pork shoulder is a very inexpensive cut that's ideal for braising—skin-on shoulder works especially well. The meat absorbs the flavor of cider which adds a touch of sweetness to balance the savory and also gives rich color to the dish.

1 **(3- to 4-lb) bone-in freshpork shoulder half (preferably arm picnic)**
2 **garlic cloves, cut into slivers**
2 **tablespoons olive oil**
1½ **lb onions (5 or 6 medium), halved lengthwise, then cut lengthwise into ¼-inch-thick slices**
¾ **cup unfiltered apple cider**

Preheat oven to 325°F.

Score fat and any skin on pork in a crosshatch pattern. Make slits all over meat with a small sharp knife and insert a garlic sliver in each slit. Pat pork dry and season with salt and pepper.

Heat oil in a 4- to 5-quart ovenproof heavy pot over moderately high heat until hot but not smoking, then brown pork on all sides, turning occasionally with tongs and a carving fork, about 8 minutes. Transfer to a plate.

Add onions to pot and sauté over moderately high heat, stirring occasionally, until softened and starting to turn golden, about 5 minutes. Add ¾ teaspoon salt and sauté onions, stirring occasionally, until golden and caramelized, 8 to 10 minutes more. Stir in cider and return pork to pot.

Cover pot with a tight-fitting lid and braise pork in middle of oven until very tender, 2½ to 3 hours.

Transfer pork to a serving dish with tongs and carving fork. Boil cooking juices with onions until reduced to about 2 cups, 2 to 3 minutes, then season with salt and black pepper and serve with pork.

Cooks' note:
• Pork can be made 1 day ahead. Cool, uncovered, then chill, covered. Reheat in liquid, covered, at 325°F about 1 hour.

Kielbasa with Sauerkraut, Mushrooms, and Onions

SERVES 4
Active time: 15 min   Start to finish: 35 min

4 tablespoons vegetable or canola oil
1 lb pork or beef kielbasa, cut diagonally into ½-inch-thick slices
1 large onion, halved and thinly sliced
10 oz cremini mushrooms, trimmed and halved (quartered if large)
2 cups drained sauerkraut (from a 16-oz package)

Heat 2 tablespoons oil in a 12-inch heavy skillet over moderately high heat until hot but not smoking, then reduce heat to moderate and sauté kielbasa, turning once, until well browned, 2 to 3 minutes on each side. Transfer to a platter. Cook onion, stirring occasionally, until golden brown, about 6 minutes. Transfer onion to kielbasa.

Add remaining 2 tablespoons oil to skillet and sauté mushrooms, stirring occasionally, until any liquid mushrooms give off is evaporated and mushrooms are browned, 8 to 10 minutes. Add ½ cup water to skillet and deglaze by simmering over high heat, stirring and scraping up any browned bits. Return kielbasa and onion to skillet, then add sauerkraut and cook over moderate heat until heated through. Season with salt and black pepper.

Currant Mustard-Glazed Ham

SERVES 6 TO 8
Active time: 35 min   Start to finish: 2¼ hr

1 (7- to 8-lb) fully cooked shank end ham
   Whole cloves for studding ham
⅓ cup red-currant jelly
1½ tablespoons Dijon mustard

Preheat oven to 350°F.

Remove any thick skin from ham and all but ⅓-inch layer of fat. Score layer of fat into diamonds, then stud center of each diamond with a clove. Put ham on a rack in a roasting pan and bake in middle of oven 55 minutes.

Heat jelly over moderate heat in a small saucepan, stirring, until melted and smooth. Remove from heat, then stir in mustard. Spoon glaze over ham, spreading evenly, and bake until glaze is brown and bubbly, 30 to 35 minutes more. Transfer ham to a platter and let stand 15 minutes before carving.

Braised Lamb with Honey and Garlic

SERVES 4
Active time: 45 min Start to finish: 2 hr

1½ lb boneless lamb shoulder, cut into
    1-inch pieces
2 tablespoons olive oil
2 tablespoons honey plus additional
    to taste
1½ tablespoons red-wine vinegar plus
    additional to taste
4 large garlic cloves, smashed

Pat lamb dry and season with salt and black pepper. Heat oil in a 4-quart heavy saucepan over moderately high heat until hot but not smoking, then brown lamb in 4 batches, stirring, about 5 minutes per batch, transferring with a slotted spoon to a bowl.

Return lamb and any accumulated juices to pot with honey, vinegar, garlic, and ¼ cup water and bring to a boil. Simmer lamb, covered, stirring occasionally until very tender, about 1¼ hours.

Season lamb with salt and black pepper and, if desired, stir in additional honey and vinegar to taste.

Lamb Chops with Coarse-Grain Mustard

SERVES 4
Active time: 15 min Start to finish: 15 min

4 (¾-inch-thick) lamb shoulder arm
    (round bone) chops, trimmed
    (2 lb total)
¼ cup coarse-grain mustard

Accompaniment: potato, red pepper, and fennel salad (page 123)

Prepare grill for cooking or heat a well-seasoned ridged grill pan (preferably cast-iron) over moderately high heat until hot.

Pat chops dry and season with salt and black pepper. Grill until undersides are browned, about 3 minutes, then turn over and spread browned sides with mustard. Grill about 4 minutes more for medium-rare.

Cooks' notes:
• To prevent chops from curling while grilling, make two ¼-inch cuts in outer curved edge of each chop.
• Grill is hot when you can hold your hand 5 inches above the rack for 1 to 2 seconds.

Veal Paprikas

SERVES 6
Active time: 30 min   Start to finish: 2 hr

1½ lb veal shoulder, cut into 1-inch cubes
 3 tablespoons olive oil
 1 large onion, halved lengthwise and cut
    into ¼-inch wedges
 2 large red bell peppers, halved,
    seeded, and cut lengthwise into
    ¼-inch-thick strips
1½ teaspoons sweet paprika
    (preferably Hungarian)

Pat veal dry and sprinkle with 1 teaspoon salt and ½ teaspoon black pepper.

Heat ½ tablespoon oil in a 3- to 4-quart heavy saucepan over moderately high heat until hot but not smoking, then brown veal in 4 batches, adding ½ tablespoon oil per batch, and transfer veal to a bowl.

Sauté onion and bell pepper in remaining tablespoon oil in saucepan over moderately high heat until softened and beginning to brown, 7 to 8 minutes. Add paprika and salt and pepper to taste and cook, stirring, 1 minute. Add veal and any accumulated juices and 2 cups water and bring to a simmer. Reduce heat and simmer gently, covered, until veal is very tender, about 2 hours. Season with salt and black pepper.

Cooks' note:
• Like all stews, veal paprikas tastes even better if made 1 day ahead. Cool, uncovered, then chill, covered.

Pounded Veal Chop with Arugula Salad

SERVES 2 GENEROUSLY
Active time: 10 min   Start to finish: 25 min

 2 (1½-inch-thick) rib veal chops
2½ tablespoons olive oil
 1 cup grape tomatoes, halved lengthwise
 1 bunch arugula (¾ lb)
 ½ tablespoon red-wine vinegar

Pound veal to a ½-inch thickness between 2 sheets of plastic wrap with a meat pounder or rolling pin and season with salt and black pepper.

Heat oil in a 12-inch heavy skillet over moderately high heat until hot but not smoking, then cook chops, turning once, until an instant-read thermometer inserted horizontally into chops registers 160°F, about 14 minutes. Transfer chops to a platter, reserving skillet, and keep warm, covered. Add tomatoes to skillet and cook over moderate heat, stirring, until slightly wilted, about 30 seconds. Remove from heat.

Toss arugula with vinegar and salt and black pepper to taste in a bowl. Add tomatoes and gently toss to combine.

Serve chops topped with arugula salad.

Weiner Schnitzel with Spaetzle

SERVES 4

Active time: 30 min   Start to finish: 45 min

1½ **lb veal cutlets (also called scallopini)**
 4 **large eggs**
1½ **cups plain dry bread crumbs**
 3 **cups all-purpose flour**
 1 **stick (½ cup) unsalted butter**

Prepare cutlets:

Pound veal to a ⅛-inch thickness between 2 sheets of plastic wrap with a meat pounder or rolling pin. Lightly beat 2 eggs in a bowl. Stir together bread crumbs and ½ teaspoon salt in a pie plate and put ½ cup flour in another pie plate or dinner plate.

Preheat oven to 200°F.

Heat 2 tablespoons butter in a 12-inch skillet over moderately high heat until foam subsides. Dredge cutlets in flour, egg, then bread crumbs, shaking off excess. Cook cutlets in 3 batches (adding 2 tablespoons butter per batch), turning once, until golden, about 4 minutes total. Wipe skillet with paper towels between batches. Transfer cooked cutlets to a platter lined with paper towels to drain, then keep warm in oven.

Make spaetzle:

Bring a large pot of salted water to a simmer. Stir together remaining 2 eggs, 1½ cups water, ½ teaspoon salt, and remaining 2½ cups flour in a bowl until smooth.

Press mixture through a colander (not a sieve) with a rubber spatula into simmering water (or use a spaetzlemaker set over pot; see below) and cook spaetzle until firm, about 3 minutes. Drain and toss with remaining 2 tablespoons butter and salt to taste.

There are numerous ways to form spaetzle (*shpets-leh*), like using a colander, but spaetzlemakers make it easy. There are two kinds you can buy and I own them both. For one, you pour the batter into the hopper and slide it back and forth, like a trolley, over boiling water—the batter falls through the holes getting cut off with each pass (available from Bridge Kitchenware, 800-274-3435 or 212-838-1901). The other is a rotary contraption which holds more batter and works like a food mill (Otto's, 818-845-0433). Some call spaetzle the pasta of Germany, but I still think of them as dumplings. (*Spatz* means "sparrow" in German. And the rounded shapelessness of the spaetzle I make resembles birds more than noodles.) I judge all spaetzle by their lightness, and those served with our wiener schnitzel practically take flight. —ZANNE STEWART

spaetzle

Soups

We've included a nice mix of hot and chilled soups because we know it's the ultimate comfort food in any kind of weather. Our garlic soup is sure to become a new wintertime cure-all, and the fresh mango and cucumber soup is destined to be a summer staple. Soup can be as versatile as you want: A modest serving can rev up an appetite at the start of a meal; a generous portion served with bread makes a satisfying one-dish dinner. And of course, soup and salad is a lunchtime favorite. All our recipes give a cup-measurement yield (as a guide, 1 cup is typically an appetizer portion). How and when you serve the soup is entirely up to you.

Butternut Squash
Chipotle Soup

MAKES ABOUT 8 CUPS
Active time: 30 min   Start to finish: 1¼ hr

1 (2¼-lb) butternut squash, halved
   lengthwise, seeded, peeled, and cut
   into ½-inch pieces
1 medium onion, chopped
1 teaspoon minced canned *chipotle* chile
   in *adobo* plus additional *adobo* sauce
   for drizzling
2 cups chicken broth
½ cup heavy cream

Bring squash, onion, chile, broth, and 3 cups
water to a boil in a large heavy saucepan over
high heat. Reduce heat to moderately low and
simmer, partially covered, stirring occasionally,
until squash is very tender and falling apart,
25 to 30 minutes.

Purée soup in batches in a blender (use caution
when blending hot liquids) and transfer to
cleaned pan. Stir in cream and salt to taste and
heat, stirring, until hot.

Divide soup among bowls and drizzle each
serving with additional *adobo* sauce.

Potato Leek Soup

MAKES ABOUT 8½ CUPS
Active time: 15 min   Start to finish: 45 min

6 medium leeks (2½ lb; white and pale
   green parts only), halved lengthwise
   and chopped
2 tablespoons unsalted butter
2 medium russet (baking) potatoes
   (1 lb), peeled and cut into
   ½-inch pieces
5 cups chicken broth
½ cup heavy cream

Wash leeks well in a bowl of cold water, then
lift out and drain well in a sieve. Cook leeks in
butter in a 5-quart heavy pot over moderate heat,
stirring occasionally, until softened, 8 to 10
minutes. Add potatoes and cook over moderately
low heat, stirring, 5 minutes. Add broth and
½ teaspoon salt and simmer, covered, until
vegetables are very tender, about 30 minutes.

Purée soup in batches in a blender until very
smooth (use caution when blending hot liquids),
then return soup to pot and stir in cream and
¼ teaspoon black pepper. Season with salt
if necessary.

Caldo Verde

MAKES ABOUT 8 CUPS
Active time: 15 min   Start to finish: 40 min

2   tablespoons olive oil
4   garlic cloves, finely chopped
**2   lb boiling potatoes (6 medium), peeled
     and cut into 2-inch pieces**
2   (14½-oz) cans chicken broth
**1   lb kale, stems and tough ribs discarded
     and leaves thinly sliced**

Heat oil in a 5-quart saucepan over moderate heat until hot but not smoking, then cook garlic, stirring, until pale golden, about 2 minutes. Add potatoes, broth, and 4 cups water. Bring to a boil, then simmer, covered, until potatoes are tender, about 15 minutes.

Remove pan from heat and coarsely mash potatoes with a potato masher (potatoes should have pea-size lumps). Stir in kale and cook over moderate heat, stirring occasionally, until tender, 6 to 8 minutes. Season with salt and black pepper.

Garlic Soup with Tortillas and Lime

MAKES ABOUT 4 CUPS
Active time: 20 min   Start to finish: 25 min

**6   large garlic cloves, thinly sliced
     (⅓ cup)**
1   tablespoon olive oil
1   qt chicken broth
4   corn tortillas
1   lime, quartered

Cook garlic in oil in a 3-quart heavy saucepan over low heat, stirring occasionally, until tender and pale golden, about 7 minutes. Add broth and bring to a simmer, then stir in ¼ teaspoon salt and ⅛ teaspoon black pepper.

While soup is heating, toast tortillas directly on burner (gas or electric) over moderately low heat, turning once with tongs, until browned in spots and crisp, 2 to 3 minutes. Cool tortillas, then break into pieces and divide among serving bowls. Ladle soup into bowls and serve with lime wedges.

chicken broth

We're strong advocates of making chicken stock from scratch—it's not hard to do and the stock freezes beautifully—but that, of course, involves planning ahead. Well, nobody's perfect. Sometimes the sheer convenience of commercial stock (or "broth," as it's usually labeled) is providential, which is why everyone we know has a stash. Since we were tasting purely for flavor, we decided to try both regular and reduced-fat and/or reduced-sodium versions. We made a sweep of our local stores and returned with the following brands: in cans—Swanson, College Inn, Campbell's, Cento, Manischewitz; in aseptic containers—Kitchen Basics, Imagine, Pacific, Health Valley; in cubes—Herb-Ox, Maggi, Wyler's, and Knorr; in concentrated form— Fond de Poulet Gold. When stacked up against homemade stock—which was robust, with a clean aftertaste—no commercial brand was a clear winner, but College Inn (reduced fat and sodium) and Swanson (regular) led the pack. The chief complaints about the others were weak flavor, excessive saltiness, and/or a chemical aftertaste. —JANE DANIELS LEAR

Mushroom Soup with Dill

MAKES ABOUT 3 CUPS
Active time: 30 min   Start to finish: 40 min

Any type of dried mushroom can be used for this soup—porcinis are readily available at your supermarket. We used packaged dried Chilean mushrooms that had a lovely smoky flavor.

- 1 **(1-oz) package dried mushrooms**
- 1 **large onion, finely chopped**
- 2½ **tablespoons unsalted butter**
- 2 **tablespoons chopped fresh dill**
- 8 **teaspoons sour cream (optional)**

Soak mushrooms in 4 cups boiling water until softened, about 20 minutes. Lift mushrooms out of soaking liquid, squeezing excess back into bowl, and rinse well to remove any grit. Drain, then pat dry and finely chop. Pour soaking liquid through a paper-towel-lined sieve into a bowl and set aside.

While mushrooms are soaking, cook onion in butter in a 2-quart heavy saucepan over moderate heat, stirring occasionally, until onions are browned well, 10 to 12 minutes. Add mushrooms, soaking liquid, and 1 tablespoon chopped dill, then simmer, uncovered, 10 minutes. Stir in ½ teaspoon salt and ⅛ teaspoon black pepper.

Divide soup among serving bowls and top each with sour cream and remaining tablespoon chopped dill.

Roasted Tomato Soup with Goat Cheese Croûtes

MAKES ABOUT 5 CUPS
Active time: 25 min   Start to finish: 1½ hr

- 6 **tablespoons extra-virgin olive oil**
- 4 **lb plum tomatoes, halved lengthwise**
- 2 **tablespoons chopped fresh basil**
- 18 **(¼-inch-thick) slices French bread (3 inches in diameter)**
- 3 **oz soft mild goat cheese at room temperature**

Garnish: chopped fresh basil

Preheat oven to 400°F.

Brush 1 tablespoon oil in each of 2 shallow baking pans. Divide tomatoes between pans, arranging cut sides up, then sprinkle with 1½ teaspoons salt and ½ teaspoon black pepper. Roast in upper and lower thirds of oven, switching position of pans halfway through baking, 1 hour total.

Purée tomatoes in batches with 2 tablespoons oil and basil in a food processor until smooth. Transfer purée to a 4-quart saucepan with 2 cups water and simmer, stirring occasionally, about 5 minutes. Add more water to thin soup to desired consistency and season with salt and black pepper. Remove from heat and keep hot, covered.

Preheat broiler.

Brush bread slices on 1 side with remaining 2 tablespoons oil and arrange, oiled sides up, in a shallow baking pan. Toast bread under broiler until edges are golden, about 1 minute. Spread tops of toasts evenly with goat cheese and heat under broiler until cheese begins to melt, about 2 minutes.

Ladle soup into bowls and top with croûtes.

Corn and Garlic Soup

MAKES ABOUT 10 CUPS
Active time: 30 min   Start to finish: 45 min

In season, fresh corn is always preferable to frozen. However, out of season it tends to lack juiciness and flavor, in which case frozen kernels are actually a better choice.

- **2   medium Yukon Gold potatoes, peeled and cut into ⅓-inch dice**
- **4   cups fresh corn kernels (5 ears) or 2 (10-oz) boxes frozen corn kernels**
- **¼   cup chopped garlic (10 cloves)**
- **½   cup thinly sliced scallion greens**

Bring potatoes, corn, garlic, and 8 cups water to a boil in a 5-quart saucepan, then reduce heat to moderately low and simmer, stirring occasionally, until potatoes are very tender, about 15 minutes.

Purée 6 cups of soup in batches in a blender (use caution when blending hot liquids), then stir into remaining soup with scallions, 2 teaspoons salt, and ½ teaspoon black pepper.

Red Bean and Ham Soup

MAKES ABOUT 8 CUPS
Active time: 20 min   Start to finish: 1¾ hr

- **1½ cups dried red kidney beans (10 oz)**
- **3   bunches scallions**
- **1   green bell pepper, chopped**
- **½   lb ham steak, cut into ½-inch pieces**
- **1   tablespoon balsamic or Sherry vinegar, or to taste**

Cover dried beans with cold water by 2 inches in a 3-quart heavy saucepan and bring to a boil. Remove from heat and soak beans, covered, 1 hour. Drain in a colander and rinse.

While beans are soaking, chop enough white and pale green parts of scallions to measure ½ cup, then thinly slice enough greens to measure ½ cup (reserve remainder for another use).

Bring beans, 5 cups water, white and pale green parts of scallion, and bell pepper to a boil, then reduce heat to moderately low and simmer, partially covered, stirring occasionally, until beans are very tender, 25 to 30 minutes.

Purée 2 cups soup in a blender (use caution when blending hot liquids), then stir purée, ham, scallion greens, and vinegar into remaining soup and season with salt and black pepper.

Cream of Cauliflower Soup with Bacon

MAKES ABOUT 6 CUPS
Active time: 25 min   Start to finish: 45 min

1 (2½-lb) head cauliflower, cut into florets
1 teaspoon cumin seeds
5 bacon slices, cut crosswise into ¼-inch-wide pieces
½ cup heavy cream

Bring cauliflower, 5 cups water, 1 teaspoon salt (or to taste), and ¼ teaspoon black pepper to a boil in a 4-quart heavy saucepan, then simmer, covered, until tender, about 15 minutes.

While cauliflower is cooking, toast cumin seeds in a small dry heavy skillet over moderate heat until fragrant, about 2 minutes. Finely grind cumin seeds in an electric coffee/spice grinder or with a mortar and pestle. Cook bacon in a 10-inch heavy skillet over moderate heat, stirring, until crisp, about 7 minutes. Transfer with a slotted spoon to paper towels to drain.

Purée cauliflower with cooking liquid and cumin in batches in a blender (use caution when blending hot liquids) until smooth. Return soup to pan and bring to a simmer, then stir in cream and salt and black pepper to taste.

Serve soup sprinkled with bacon.

Carrot Ginger Soup

MAKES ABOUT 9 CUPS
Active time: 15 min   Start to finish: 45 min

½ stick (¼ cup) unsalted butter
4 large shallots, chopped (1½ cups)
8 medium carrots (1½ lb), chopped
1 (2-inch) piece peeled fresh ginger, finely chopped
½ cup unsweetened coconut milk

Heat butter in a 5-quart pot over moderate heat until foam subsides, then cook shallots, stirring occasionally, until golden, 8 to 10 minutes. Add chopped carrots and ginger and cook, covered, until carrots are softened but not browned, about 10 minutes. Add 5 cups water and 2 teaspoons salt and simmer, covered, until carrots are very tender, about 25 minutes. Purée soup in batches in a blender until smooth (use caution when blending hot liquids), then return to pot and stir in coconut milk and ¼ teaspoon black pepper. Season with salt if necessary.

Chilled Tomato, Basil, and Goat Cheese Soup

MAKES ABOUT 3 CUPS
Active time: 10 min Start to finish: 1¼ hr

1 (14- to 15-oz) can stewed tomatoes, chilled for 1 hour
2 oz soft mild goat cheese (¼ cup)
2 tablespoons extra-virgin olive oil
¼ cup coarsely chopped fresh basil

Blend all ingredients with ¾ cup water, ¾ teaspoon salt, and ½ teaspoon black pepper in a blender until smooth. Serve soup chilled.

fresh mango and cucumber soup

Fresh Mango and Cucumber Soup

MAKES ABOUT 7 CUPS
Active time: 30 min   Start to finish: 45 min

2 mangoes, peeled and pitted (2 lb total)
2 seedless cucumbers (usually
    plastic-wrapped; 1½ lb total)
3 tablespoons finely chopped red onion
3 tablespoons fresh lime juice, or to taste
2 tablespoons chopped fresh cilantro

Finely chop 1 mango and 1 cucumber and set aside. Coarsely chop remaining mango and cucumber and purée with ¼ cup water in a blender until almost smooth. Transfer to a bowl and stir in finely chopped mango and cucumber, onion, lime juice, and 2 cups cold water. Place bowl in a larger bowl of ice and cold water and stir until cool. Just before serving, stir in cilantro and 1¼ teaspoons salt.

Cooks' note:
• Soup can also be chilled in the refrigerator until cold, but it will take about 2 hours.

Cucumber and Cumin Soup

MAKES ABOUT 3 CUPS
Active time: 15 min   Start to finish: 1¼ hr

¼ teaspoon cumin seeds
2 cucumbers (¾ lb total), peeled, seeded,
    and cut into pieces
1 small garlic clove, chopped
¾ cup well-shaken buttermilk

Toast seeds in a dry heavy skillet over moderate heat, stirring, until fragrant and a shade or two darker. Blend all ingredients in a blender until smooth, then transfer to a bowl and season with salt and black pepper. Chill soup, covered, until cold, about 1 hour.

Chilled Celery Consommé

MAKES ABOUT 3 CUPS
Active time: 20 min   Start to finish: 3½ hr

2 large Granny Smith apples
1 large cucumber
4 teaspoons fresh lemon juice plus
    additional to taste
3 cups coarsely chopped celery,
    leaves reserved for garnish
1 teaspoon unflavored gelatin

Finely dice enough apple and cucumber to measure 3 tablespoons each, then sprinkle dice with 1 teaspoon lemon juice and reserve for garnish, covered and chilled. Coarsely chop remaining apple and cucumber and purée with celery, 3 teaspoons lemon juice, 1¼ cups water, and 2 teaspoons salt in batches in a blender until very smooth, about 2 minutes. Pour through a large fine sieve into a bowl. Drain 15 minutes without disturbing, then discard solids.

Sprinkle gelatin over ¼ cup cold water in a small heavy saucepan and let soften 1 minute. Heat gelatin over low heat, stirring until dissolved. Stir gelatin into vegetable juice and season with salt, black pepper, and additional lemon juice. Chill, covered, until thickened, at least 3 hours. Garnish with celery leaves and finely diced apple and cucumber.

Cooks' note:
• Consommé and garnish can chill, covered separately, up to 1 day ahead.

Side Dishes

everyone knows a superhero is only as good as his sidekick. So when you can't decide what to serve with a main dish, look here for a few of our trusty favorites, like leeks braised in white wine, fennel mashed potatoes, or broccoli sautéed with garlic and ginger. Team up French-fried onion rings (some of the best we've ever tasted) with burgers and sandwiches. Pair our corn bread supreme with any soup to make a truly dynamic duo. Need something a bit more elegant? Try our zucchini parmesan fritters or luscious sautéed cabbage and cream—they're knockouts.

Carrot and Radish Salad

SERVES 4
Active time: 15 min   Start to finish: 15 min

*This wonderfully versatile salad can be served
with almost any main course any time of the year.
The vinaigrette is zesty and fresh, yet it's mild
enough to work well with a variety of flavors.*

- 4 medium carrots
- 6 large radishes
- ¼ teaspoon finely grated fresh lime zest
- 1 tablespoon fresh lime juice
- 1½ tablespoons olive oil

Shred carrots with a *mandoline* or other
manual slicer or in a food processor fitted with
shredding disk. Julienne radishes. Whisk together
zest, juice, oil, and salt and black pepper to taste
and toss with vegetables.

Sautéed Cabbage with Bacon and Cream

SERVES 4
Active time: 15 min   Start to finish: 25 min

- ¼ lb sliced bacon, cut crosswise into
     ½-inch pieces
- 1 small head cabbage (2 lb), cored and
     coarsely shredded (10 cups)
- ½ cup heavy cream

Cook bacon in a deep 12-inch heavy skillet
over moderately high heat, stirring, until golden,
3 to 4 minutes. Add cabbage and 1 teaspoon salt
and cook over moderate heat, stirring, until
cabbage is wilted, about 3 minutes. Add cream
and cook, covered, over moderately low heat,
stirring occasionally, until cabbage is tender and
creamy, 10 to 15 minutes more. Season with salt
and black pepper.

Jerusalem Artichoke Purée with Sage and Parmesan

SERVES 4
Active time: 20 min   Start to finish: 40 min

1½ lb Jerusalem artichokes, peeled
    and cut into ½-inch pieces
1 cup skim milk
¼ cup finely grated parmesan
1 teaspoon finely chopped fresh sage

Simmer artichokes in skim milk in a heavy 3-quart saucepan, covered, until tender, about 15 minutes.

Purée artichokes, milk, parmesan, and sage in a food processor until smooth, then season with salt and black pepper.

Fried Potatoes

SERVES 4
Active time: 30 min   Start to finish: 40 min

2 lb large Yukon Gold potatoes
3 cups olive oil
    Sea salt to taste

Special equipment: a deep-fat thermometer

Peel potatoes and cut into 4- by ½-inch sticks, transferring as cut to a bowl of cold water. Drain potatoes in a colander and pat dry between sheets of paper towels.

Heat oil in a deep 12-inch heavy skillet over moderately high heat until it registers 360°F on thermometer, then fry one fourth of potatoes, stirring occasionally, until golden brown, 5 to 7 minutes. Transfer potatoes with a slotted spoon to paper towels to drain and season with salt. Fry remaining potatoes in same manner, returning oil to 360°F between batches. Serve immediately.

Rutabaga and Carrot Purée

SERVES 8
Active time: 15 min   Start to finish: 50 min

2 rutabagas (2½ lb total), peeled and cut
    into 1-inch pieces
5 carrots, cut into 1-inch pieces
3 tablespoons unsalted butter
3 tablespoons packed light brown sugar
1 teaspoon kosher salt

Cook rutabagas and carrots in boiling salted water to cover by 1 inch in a large pot until tender, about 30 minutes. Transfer vegetables with a slotted spoon to a food processor and purée with butter, brown sugar, and kosher salt until very smooth. If necessary, transfer purée back to pot and reheat.

Cooks' note:
• Purée keeps 3 days, covered and chilled.

Corn Bread Supreme

SERVES 6 TO 8
Active time: 5 min   Start to finish: 1 hr

We find corn breads are often dry, but this one from Mary Anne Dekle in Staunton, Virginia, is exceptionally creamy and moist.

2 large eggs
1 (8-oz) container sour cream
1 (8-oz) can creamed corn
½ cup vegetable oil
1 cup self-rising cornmeal mix
    (not corn-bread mix)

Preheat oven to 425°F.

Whisk together eggs, sour cream, corn, and oil, then whisk in cornmeal until just combined (do not overmix). Pour batter into a buttered and floured 8-inch square baking pan, spreading evenly, and bake in middle of oven until lightly browned, about 30 minutes. Cool in pan on a rack before cutting into pieces.

Sautéed Cauliflower with Anchovies

SERVES 6
Active time: 10 min   Start to finish: 20 min

1 (2¼-lb) head cauliflower, cut into
    small florets
3 flat anchovies, drained and patted dry
1 garlic clove, finely chopped
3 tablespoons olive oil

Steam cauliflower in a steamer basket or large colander over boiling water, covered, until just tender, about 4 minutes.

While cauliflower is steaming, mash anchovies to a paste with a fork. Cook garlic in oil in a 12-inch nonstick skillet over moderate heat, stirring, until pale golden, then add anchovies and cook, stirring, 1 minute.

Add cauliflower and cook, stirring, until coated with anchovies, then season with salt and black pepper.

Stir-Fried Broccoli with Garlic and Ginger

SERVES 4
Active time: 15 min   Start to finish: 18 min

1 **bunch broccoli (1½ lb)**
2 **tablespoons vegetable oil**
1 **tablespoon minced garlic**
1 **tablespoon minced peeled fresh ginger**
½ **cup chicken broth**

Remove stems from broccoli, then peel them and cut diagonally into ½-inch pieces. Cut head into small florets.

Heat a wok or 12-inch heavy skillet over moderately high heat until a bead of water dropped on cooking surface evaporates immediately. Add oil, swirling wok to coat evenly, and heat until just beginning to smoke. Stir-fry garlic, ginger, and ¼ teaspoon salt until fragrant, about 30 seconds. Add broccoli stems and stir-fry 3 minutes, then add florets and stir-fry 2 minutes. Stir in broth, then cover and cook just until broccoli is crisp-tender, 3 to 4 minutes. Uncover and cook just until liquid is evaporated, about 1 minute more.

Zucchini Parmesan Fritters

SERVES 6
Active time: 20 min   Start to finish: 40 min

1¼ **lb zucchini, coarsely grated**
1 **large egg**
⅓ **cup grated parmesan (1 oz)**
⅓ **cup plain fine dry bread crumbs (1¼ oz)**
  About ⅓ cup vegetable oil

Preheat oven to 200°F.

Toss grated zucchini with 1 teaspoon salt in a colander and let stand 30 minutes. Squeeze handfuls of zucchini in a clean kitchen towel to remove as much moisture as possible.

Lightly beat egg in a bowl, then stir in zucchini, cheese, bread crumbs, and ¼ teaspoon black pepper.

Heat 3 tablespoons oil in a 12-inch nonstick skillet over moderate heat until hot but not smoking. Working in batches of 5, drop 1 rounded tablespoon batter for each fritter into hot oil, then flatten fritters with a fork and cook until undersides are golden, about 2 minutes. Turn fritters over with a spatula and cook until golden, about 2 minutes more, and transfer to paper towels to drain. Keep warm in oven while making more fritters, adding more oil to skillet as needed.

Crisp Rosemary Potatoes

SERVES 4
Active time: 15 min   Start to finish: 35 min

Think of these as a cross between potato chips and roasted potatoes. They'd be a perfect side dish for a variety of main courses (especially those with sauces—they're made for dipping) or, better still, as a crisp alternative for plain boiled potatoes in a salade niçoise.

**2 lb red potatoes, cut into
    ¼-inch-thick slices
1 tablespoon olive oil
2 tablespoons chopped fresh rosemary**

Preheat oven to 450°F.

Arrange potatoes in 1 layer on 2 generously oiled baking sheets. Brush tops of potatoes with oil and sprinkle with rosemary and salt and black pepper to taste.

Roast potatoes in upper and lower thirds of oven, switching position of sheets halfway through baking, until golden and edges are crisp, about 20 minutes.

Glazed Turnips

SERVES 4
Active time: 20 min   Start to finish: 35 min

These sweet glazed turnips make an exceptionally nice side dish for roasted meats or poultry.

**2 lb small to medium (2-inch) turnips
2 tablespoons butter
1 tablespoon sugar**

Garnish: chopped fresh flat-leaf parsley

Peel turnips, then halve crosswise and quarter halves. Arrange turnips in 1 layer in a 12-inch heavy skillet and add enough water (about 1½ cups) to reach halfway up turnips. Add butter, sugar, and ½ teaspoon salt and boil over moderately high heat, covered, stirring occasionally, 10 minutes. Boil turnips, uncovered, stirring, until tender and water has evaporated, about 8 minutes.

Sauté turnips over moderately high heat, stirring, until golden brown, about 5 minutes more. Add 3 tablespoons water and stir to coat turnips with glaze.

glazed turnips

Fennel Mashed Potatoes

SERVES 6
Active time: 15 min   Start to finish: 55 min

2½ **lb boiling potatoes, peeled and quartered**
1½ **lb fennel bulbs (sometimes called anise; about 2 medium), with fronds**
1 **cup milk**
2 **teaspoons extra-virgin olive oil**

Cover potatoes with salted cold water by 2 inches, then simmer until very tender, about 30 minutes. Drain potatoes in a colander and transfer to a large bowl.

While potatoes cook, trim fennel stalks flush with bulbs, reserving fronds and discarding stalks. Halve bulbs and discard cores, then cut bulbs lengthwise into ¼-inch-thick slices. Chop reserved fronds. Poach sliced fennel and three fourths of fronds in milk in a large saucepan, at a bare simmer, covered, until very tender, about 30 minutes.

Purée fennel milk in a blender until smooth (use caution when blending hot liquids). Add purée to potatoes, then mash with a potato masher. Season potatoes with salt and black pepper and serve drizzled with oil and sprinkled with remaining fennel fronds.

Cooks' note:
• Potatoes can be made 1 day ahead and chilled, covered. Reheat potatoes, covered, in a 350°F oven about 30 minutes.

Potato, Red Pepper, and Fennel Salad

MAKES ABOUT 6 CUPS
Active time: 10 min   Start to finish: 30 min

1½ lb small (1½-inch) red potatoes
½ fennel bulb (sometimes called anise),
    with fronds
3 tablespoons white-wine vinegar
¼ cup extra-virgin olive oil
1 large red bell pepper, cut into
    ½-inch pieces

Simmer potatoes in salted cold water to cover by 1 inch in a large saucepan until tender, 20 to 25 minutes. Drain and rinse under cold water. When cool enough to handle, cut each potato into 8 wedges.

While potatoes are cooking, trim fennel stalks flush with bulb, discarding stalks, and chop enough fronds to measure 2 tablespoons. Remove core and cut bulb into ½-inch pieces.

Whisk together vinegar, oil, and salt and black pepper to taste in a large bowl. Add warm potatoes, fennel bulb and fronds, and bell pepper, then toss well. Season with salt and black pepper.

Beet Salad with Dill and Sour Cream

SERVES 4
Active time: 15 min   Start to finish: 15 min

¼ cup finely chopped red onion
2 tablespoons sour cream
1 tablespoon fresh lemon juice,
    or to taste
2 (14- to 15-oz) cans small whole beets,
    drained and each cut into
    4 to 6 wedges
2 tablespoons chopped fresh dill

Stir together onion, sour cream, lemon juice, 2 teaspoons water, and salt and black pepper to taste in a bowl, then stir in beets and dill.

French-Fried Onion Rings

SERVES 4
Active time: 10 min   Start to finish: 30 min

6 cups vegetable oil
1 large onion (1 lb), cut crosswise
    into ¼-inch slices
1 cup whole milk
1½ cups all-purpose flour

Accompaniment: ketchup
Special equipment: a deep-fat thermometer

Heat oil in a 4- to 5-quart saucepan until it registers 370°F on thermometer. Separate onion slices into rings. Pour milk into a bowl and combine flour and ½ teaspoon salt in a pie plate.

Dip 3 onion rings alternately into milk and flour twice, transferring rings to oil as coated. Fry rings, stirring until golden, about 2 minutes, and transfer with tongs to paper towels to drain. Coat and fry more rings in same manner, returning oil to 370°F between batches. Serve immediately.

Orzo, Radish, and Chive Salad

SERVES 2
Active time: 10 min   Start to finish: 20 min

- ½ cup orzo
- 1½ tablespoons mayonnaise
- 2 teaspoons fresh lemon juice
- 4 radishes, quartered and thinly sliced
- 1 tablespoon minced fresh chives

Cook orzo in a small saucepan of boiling salted water until al dente, about 10 minutes, then drain in a sieve and rinse under cold water until cool. Drain well.

Transfer orzo to a bowl and add mayonnaise and lemon juice, stirring to coat. Stir in radishes, chives, and salt and black pepper to taste.

Braised Baby Bok Choy

SERVES 2
Active time: 15 min   Start to finish: 15 min

While at The Boathouse restaurant in Sydney, our food editors sampled a dish of baby bok choy so good that it led them to create their own version.

- 1 cup chicken broth
- 3 tablespoons unsalted butter
- ¾ lb baby bok choy, trimmed
- ½ teaspoon Asian sesame oil

Bring broth and butter to a simmer in a deep large heavy skillet. Arrange bok choy evenly in skillet and simmer, covered, until tender, about 5 minutes. Transfer bok choy with tongs to a serving dish and keep warm, covered.

Boil broth mixture until reduced to about ¼ cup, then stir in sesame oil and black pepper to taste. Pour over bok choy.

Braised Leeks

SERVES 4
Active time: 10 min Start to finish: 35 min

- 3 lb medium leeks (10; white and pale-green parts only)
- 2 tablespoons unsalted butter
- ½ cup white wine
- 3 fresh thyme sprigs
- 6 parsley stems (no leaves) plus 2 tablespoons chopped fresh flat-leaf parsley

Halve leeks lengthwise (quarter if large), then wash well under cold water and pat dry.

Heat butter in a deep 12-inch heavy skillet over moderate heat until foam subsides, then cook leeks, turning once, until golden but not cooked through, 6 to 8 minutes. Add wine and cook until liquid is reduced by half, about 3 minutes. Add thyme, parsley stems, 2 cups water, ¾ teaspoon salt, and ½ teaspoon whole black peppercorns and cook, partially covered, until leeks are tender, 16 to 18 minutes.

Transfer leeks with tongs to a serving plate, then increase heat to high and boil cooking liquid until reduced to a light syrup, about 3 minutes. Pour sauce through a fine sieve onto leeks and sprinkle with chopped parsley.

Roasted Brussels Sprouts with Garlic and Pancetta

SERVES 4
Active time: 10 min   Start to finish: 35 min

1 lb Brussels sprouts, trimmed and halved (quartered if large)
2 oz pancetta (visible fat discarded), minced
1 garlic clove, minced
½ tablespoon extra-virgin olive oil

Preheat oven to 450°F.

Toss together Brussels sprouts, pancetta, garlic, oil, and salt and black pepper to taste in an 11- by 7-inch baking pan and spread in 1 layer.

Roast in upper third of oven, stirring once halfway through roasting, until sprouts are brown on edges and tender, about 25 minutes total. Stir in ¼ cup water, scraping up brown bits. Serve warm.

Green Beans with Lemon

SERVES 8
Active time: 20 min   Start to finish: 25 min

2½ lb *haricots verts* or other thin green beans, trimmed
1 tablespoon unsalted butter
½ teaspoon finely grated fresh lemon zest

Cook beans in a large pot of boiling salted water until crisp-tender, 4 to 6 minutes. Drain beans and toss with butter, zest, and salt to taste.

zester

Who knew that Microplane's woodworking rasp would morph into an incredible cooking tool? The reason lies in its cutting edges: They're sharp as tiny razors. We prefer the Microplane to the tiny "knuckle buster" holes on a box grater: Gently sweeping a lemon across its easy-to-clean surface yields dry, fluffy shards of zest. One point: It produces a greater volume of zest, so pack it if measuring. You'll find a variety of models available at many cookware shops and from Lee Valley Tools (800-871-8158). —JANE DANIELS LEAR

Snacks

gone are the days of running to the store for a bag of chips when the munchies strike. Our almond, raisin, coconut, and granola snack mix (gorp) is completely addictive and takes only 15 minutes to prepare. The spicy peanuts and popcorn; potato chips; and baked pear chips with cinnamon are more time consuming, but they're equally delicious and keep for a week. When you crave something more substantial, we oblige with speedy pizzas and pita pockets stuffed with cucumber, black olives, and feta. And if your idea of a snack is a bit more refined, there's even a collection of goodies to serve with afternoon tea.

Gorp

MAKES ABOUT 6 CUPS
Active time: 10 min   Start to finish: 15 min

*Gorp (also known as snack mix or trail mix) is
an acronym for "good old raisins and peanuts"
(our version has almonds and coconut). It's
a satisfying treat that travels extremely well.*

     3 **tablespoons unsalted butter**
    1½ **cups whole almonds (9 oz)**
    1½ **cups raisins**
     1 **cup sweetened flaked coconut**
     2 **cups plain granola**

Preheat oven to 350°F.

Heat butter in a 12-inch heavy skillet over
moderate heat until foam subsides, then toast
almonds in butter, stirring, until golden brown,
about 5 minutes. Transfer with a slotted spoon
to paper towels to drain, reserving skillet, and
season with salt. When almonds are cool, transfer
to a large bowl.

Cook raisins in skillet, stirring, over moderate
heat until softened, about 2 minutes. Add raisins
to almonds.

Spread coconut in a shallow baking pan and
toast in middle of oven, stirring occasionally,
until golden, 5 to 8 minutes. Cool coconut and
add to almonds and raisins, then toss with plain
granola. Season gorp with salt.

Cooks' note:
• Gorp keeps 1 week in an airtight container.

Potato Chips

SERVES 4
Active time: 1½ hr   Start to finish: 1½ hr

*This recipe was inspired by the wonderful
handmade chips once served in the bar of the
Hôtel Lancaster in Paris.*

     4 **russet (baking) potatoes (2 lb)**
        About 4 cups canola oil for deep-frying

Special equipment: *a mandoline* or other
    manual slicer; a deep-fat thermometer

Peel potatoes and put in a bowl of cold water
to cover. Pat 1 potato dry and cut crosswise into
paper-thin slices (about ¹⁄₁₆-inch thick) with
mandoline. Transfer slices to another bowl of
cold water and let stand 5 minutes.

Drain slices well and arrange (without
overlapping) on a triple layer of paper towels.
Blot slices completely dry with another triple
layer of paper towels.

Heat oil in a 3-quart saucepan until it registers
380°F on thermometer. Fry potatoes in batches of
8 to 10 slices, turning once or twice, until golden,
1½ to 2 minutes, then transfer chips with a large
slotted spoon to paper towels to drain. (Return oil
to 380°F between batches.) Season chips with
salt. Pat dry, cut, dry, and fry remaining potatoes
in same manner.

Cooks' note:
• Potato chips can be made 2 days ahead and kept
  in an airtight container at room temperature.

Baked Pear Chips with Cinnamon

MAKES ABOUT 20 CHIPS
Active time: 10 min   Start to finish: 2½ hr

¼ cup confectioners sugar
1 teaspoon cinnamon
2 firm-ripe Bosc pears

Special equipment: a nonstick baking
    pad such as Silpat or parchment paper;
    a mandoline or other adjustable-blade
    slicer

Preheat oven to 200°F and line a large baking sheet with baking pad or parchment.

Sift together confectioners sugar and cinnamon to incorporate, then sift half of cinnamon-sugar evenly onto baking sheet.

Cut pears lengthwise into very thin slices (about ¹⁄₁₆ -inch thick) with *mandoline*. Arrange 20 of largest slices nearly touching each other on baking sheet, then evenly sift remaining cinnamon-sugar over pears. (Reserve remaining pear slices for another use.)

Bake slices in middle of oven until pale golden and beginning to crisp on edges, about 2¼ hours. Immediately peel chips off baking pad and cool on a rack.

Cooks' note:
• Pear chips keep 1 week in an airtight container at room temperature.

Spicy Peanuts and Popcorn

MAKES ABOUT 10 CUPS
Active time: 10 min   Start to finish: 30 min

8 cups packaged buttered popcorn
    (3½ oz)
2 cups roasted salted peanuts (8 oz)
3 tablespoons unsalted butter, melted
2 tablespoons sugar
½ to ¾ teaspoon cayenne

Preheat oven to 375°F.

Toss popcorn and peanuts with butter in a large bowl until coated, then sprinkle with sugar, cayenne (to taste), and ¼ teaspoon salt and toss again. Transfer to a large shallow baking pan and bake in middle of oven, stirring occasionally, until a crispy coating forms, 15 to 17 minutes. Cool completely in pan on a rack.

Cooks' note:
• Popcorn can be made 1 week ahead, kept in an airtight container.

Sesame Pita Triangles

MAKES 36 TRIANGLES
Active time: 30 min   Start to finish: 40 min

 1 lemon
 ½ cup sesame seeds, lightly toasted
 1 cup loosely packed fresh
     flat-leaf parsley
 ¼ cup extra-virgin olive oil
 3 (6- to 7-inch) pitas, split crosswise
     and each cut into 6 wedges

Preheat oven to 450°F.

Grate enough zest from lemon to measure 1 tablespoon, then squeeze enough juice to measure 1 teaspoon. Blend zest, juice, sesame seeds, parsley, 2 tablespoons oil, ½ teaspoon salt, and ¼ teaspoon black pepper in a blender until a crumbly paste forms, scraping down side of blender often.

Brush cut sides of pitas with remaining 2 tablespoons oil and spread 1 teaspoon sesame mixture onto each wedge, pressing gently to adhere. Place pitas on a large baking sheet and bake in middle of oven in 2 batches, until crisp and golden, about 8 minutes. Transfer to a rack to cool.

Spicy Cheddar Sticks

MAKES 48 STICKS
Active time: 30 min   Start to finish: 1¼ hr

 1 tablespoon paprika
 ½ to ¾ teaspoon cayenne
 1 (17¼-oz) package frozen puff pastry
     sheets, thawed
 1 large egg white, lightly beaten with
     1 teaspoon water
 ½ lb sharp Cheddar, grated (2 cups)

Preheat oven to 375°F.

Stir together paprika, cayenne (to taste), and ¼ teaspoon salt in small bowl.

Roll out 1 pastry sheet on a lightly floured surface with a lightly floured rolling pin into a 14-inch square. Brush pastry with egg white, then sprinkle half of square with half of paprika mixture and half of cheese, pressing gently to adhere. Fold pastry over filling to form a rectangle, then roll lightly with rolling pin to help layers adhere and trim edges. Cut pastry into 7- by ½-inch strips.

Arrange strips ½ inch apart on 2 greased large baking sheets, twisting each strip twice and pressing ends onto sheets. Bake in upper and lower thirds of oven until golden, about 20 minutes, and transfer twists to a rack to cool slightly. Make more cheese sticks in same manner. Serve warm.

Cooks' note:
• Reheat cheese sticks in a 350°F oven 6 minutes.

Speedy Pizzas

SERVES 4
Active time: 20 min   Start to finish: 20 min

You can personalize these quick and easy pizzas by adding your favorite toppings, such as prosciutto, basil, arugula, or roasted vegetables.

- **1 large onion, coarsely chopped**
- **1 tablespoon olive oil**
- **1 (12-oz) jar roasted red peppers, patted dry and coarsely chopped**
- **4 (7-inch) flour tortillas**
- **2 oz pepper Jack cheese or mozzarella, coarsely grated (½ cup)**

Preheat oven to 475°F.

Cook onion in oil in a large heavy skillet over moderate heat, stirring, until softened, about 6 minutes. Stir in peppers and salt and black pepper to taste.

Toast tortillas directly on burners (gas or electric) over moderately low heat, turning once with tongs, until puffed slightly and browned in spots, about 30 seconds on each side.

Arrange tortillas in 1 layer on a large baking sheet and spoon one fourth of onions and peppers onto each tortilla, leaving a ¼-inch border around edge. Sprinkle pizzas with cheese and bake in middle of oven until cheese is melted and edges of tortillas are browned, about 5 minutes. Season with black pepper.

Goat Cheese Quesadillas

SERVES 4
Active time: 20 min   Start to finish: 30 min

1   medium onion, sliced
1   tablespoon plus 2 teaspoons
      extra-virgin olive oil
4   (8-inch) flour tortillas
4   oz herbed goat cheese, softened
½   cup fresh cilantro sprigs

Cook onion in 1 tablespoon oil in a 12-inch nonstick skillet over moderate heat, stirring, until golden brown, about 15 minutes. Spread 1 side of each tortilla evenly with goat cheese, then arrange onion and cilantro over half and season with salt and black pepper. Fold tortillas over filling to form a half-moon shape.

Heat 1 teaspoon oil in cleaned skillet over moderately high heat until hot but not smoking, then cook tortillas in 2 batches, turning once, until golden brown, about 3 minutes total (add remaining teaspoon oil between batches).

Cut *quesadillas* into wedges and serve immediately.

Curry Nut Toasts

SERVES 6
Active time: 15 min   Start to finish: 30 min

12   (½-inch-thick) slices raisin bread
       (preferably semolina or sourdough)
1   stick (½ cup) unsalted butter, softened
2   teaspoons curry powder (preferably
       Madras)
½   cup finely chopped salted cashews
       (2 oz)

Preheat oven to 425°F.

Arrange bread slices in 1 layer on a large baking sheet.

Stir together butter and curry powder in a small bowl, then spread evenly on 1 side of each bread slice and sprinkle evenly with nuts.

Bake in middle of oven until toasts are bubbling and lightly golden, about 15 minutes. Serve immediately.

za'atar

Variations of *za'atar*, a sesame-thyme seasoning, can be found all over the Middle East. And a typical Israeli breakfast of tomato and cucumber salad with pita bread would not be complete without it. The warm flat bread is dunked in good olive oil and then in the spice dip. Besides pitas *za'atar* is also used to flavor eggs. Many Middle Eastern stores sell a dried version (made with dried thyme) but it just doesn't compare to *za'atar* made fresh. **To make *za'atar*:** stir together 2 tablespoons toasted sesame seeds, 2 teaspoons ground sumac, 1½ to 2 tablespoons minced fresh thyme, and ½ teaspoon salt in a small bowl. It keeps in an airtight container, chilled for 1 week.

Pita Pockets with Cucumber, Black Olive, and Feta Stuffing

MAKES 12 SMALL PITA POCKETS
Active time: 20 min   Start to finish: 50 min

Two pints of quartered cherry tomatoes can be substituted for the cucumber in this recipe. These pitas can also be served on their own, brushed with olive oil and sprinkled with coarse salt, or try them with the Middle Eastern herb and spice mix, za'atar *(see information on page 132).*

1   **lb frozen pizza dough (store-bought), thawed**
2   **cucumbers (1¼ lb), peeled, halved, and seeded**
1   **cup feta (5 oz), crumbled**
½   **cup Kalamata or other brine-cured black olives, pitted and coarsely chopped**
6   **tablespoons extra-virgin olive oil**

Special equipment: a pizza stone or 4 to 6 unglazed "quarry" tiles

At least 45 minutes before baking pizza, put a pizza stone or tiles arranged close together on oven rack in lowest position in oven and preheat oven to highest setting (500°–550°F).

Divide pizza dough into 12 pieces and form into balls. Cover with plastic wrap and let rise at room temperature until doubled in size, about 30 minutes.

While dough is rising, cut cucumbers into ¼-inch dice and toss with feta, olives, oil, and salt and black pepper to taste.

On a lightly floured surface roll out 6 dough balls into 4-inch disks, then transfer to hot pizza stone and bake, without turning, until puffed and undersides are golden, 3 to 4 minutes (pita tops will not be colored). Turn pitas over and bake 30 seconds to brown slightly. Transfer to a kitchen-towel-lined basket and keep warm, covered. Make more pitas with remaining dough.

Make a 3-inch slit on edge of each pita and fill with cucumber mixture.

Cooks' notes:
• Cucumber filling can be made 4 hours ahead, covered and chilled.
• Pita breads are best served right away, but they can be made 4 hours ahead and kept at room temperature, covered with a kitchen towel. Reheat, if desired, before serving.

Cream Drop Biscuits

MAKES 12 BISCUITS
Active time: 15 min   Start to finish: 40 min

In the mood for a real treat? Hot cream biscuits with butter and jam can be just the thing. Try them with our quick strawberry jam (recipe follows).

2½ cups all-purpose flour
1 tablespoon baking powder
1 tablespoon sugar
2 cups chilled heavy cream

Preheat oven to 400°F.

Stir together flour, baking powder, sugar, and 1 teaspoon salt in a large bowl. Add cream, then stir just until a dough forms.

Drop heaping ¼ cups batter about 1 inch apart on an ungreased large baking sheet. Bake in middle of oven until tops are pale golden and bottoms are golden brown, 18 to 20 minutes.

Quick Strawberry Jam

MAKES ABOUT 1¼ CUPS
Active time: 10 min   Start to finish: 40 min

We've given a range on the amount of sugar because some berries are sweeter than others.

1 lb fresh strawberries, trimmed
   and halved
⅔ to ¾ cup sugar
2 tablespoons powdered fruit pectin
2 teaspoons fresh lemon juice

Mash strawberries in a large bowl with a potato masher or a fork.

Stir together berries, sugar (to taste), pectin, and lemon juice in a 12-inch nonstick skillet and boil until slightly thickened, about 5 minutes. Transfer to a bowl to cool, then chill, covered, until ready to serve.

Cooks' note:
• Jam keeps 2 weeks, chilled in an airtight container.

Meyer Lemon Marmalade

MAKES 6 (½-PINT) JARS
Active time: 1¼ hr   Start to finish: 25¼ hr

6 **Meyer lemons (1½ lb)**
4 **cups sugar**

Special equipment: cheesecloth; kitchen
  string; 6 (½-pint) canning jars with lids
  and screw bands, sterilized (see below)

Halve lemons crosswise and remove seeds.
Tie seeds in a cheesecloth bag with string.
Quarter each lemon half and thinly slice, then
combine with bag of seeds and 4 cups water in a
nonreactive 5-quart heavy pot and let stand,
covered, at room temperature 24 hours.

Bring lemon mixture to a boil over moderate
heat. Reduce heat and simmer, uncovered, until
reduced to 4 cups, about 45 minutes.

Stir in sugar and boil over moderate heat,
stirring occasionally and skimming off any foam,
until a teaspoon of mixture dropped on a cold
plate gels, about 15 minutes.

Ladle hot marmalade into jars, filling to within
¼ inch of top. Wipe rims with dampened cloth
and seal jars with lids.

Put jars in a water-bath canner or on a rack set
in a deep pot. Add enough hot water to cover jars
by 1 inch and bring to a boil. Boil jars, covered,
5 minutes and transfer with tongs to a rack. Cool
jars completely.

Cooks' note:
• Marmalade keeps 1 year, stored in a cool,
  dark place.

sterilizing jars

Wash jars, lids, and screw bands in hot soapy water, then
rinse well. Dry screw bands. Put jars and lids on
a rack in a boiling-water canner or a
deep 8- to 10-quart pot and add enough
water to cover by 2 inches. Heat water until an
instant-read thermometer registers 180°F. Do not let boil.
Keep jars submerged in hot water, covered, until ready to use.

Avocado, Smoked Salmon, and Scallion Tea Sandwiches

MAKES 16 TEA SANDWICHES
Active time: 15 min   Start to finish: 15 min

1   ripe California avocado, quartered
      and peeled
¼   cup finely chopped scallion
2   teaspoons fresh lemon juice
8   slices pumpernickel sandwich
      bread, crusts discarded
¼   lb thinly sliced smoked salmon

Mash together avocado, scallion, lemon juice, and ½ teaspoon salt (or to taste) in a bowl and divide among bread slices, spreading evenly. Divide salmon among 4 bread slices, then top with remaining 4 slices, spread sides down. Cut sandwiches into quarters.

Cooks' note:
• Sandwiches can be made 1 hour ahead and chilled, covered with dampened paper towels and plastic wrap.

Pecan Cream Cheese Tea Sandwiches

MAKES 36 TEA SANDWICHES
Active time: 15 min   Start to finish: 30 min

1   cup pecans (4 oz), finely chopped
8   oz cream cheese, softened
⅓   cup finely chopped flat-leaf parsley
1   tablespoon fresh lemon juice
24 slices firm white sandwich bread,
      crusts discarded

Preheat oven to 350°F.
Toast chopped pecans on a baking sheet in middle of oven until fragrant and a shade darker, 7 to 8 minutes, then cool in a bowl. Stir together pecans, cream cheese, parsley, lemon juice, and salt and black pepper to taste in a bowl until spread is combined well.

Spread 2 tablespoons of pecan cream cheese on 1 side of each of 12 bread slices and top with remaining slices, then cut each sandwich into 3 rectangles.

Cooks' note:
• Cream cheese mixture can be made 1 day ahead, covered and chilled.

Sweets

most of us crave sweets. In a pinch, a scoop of store-bought ice cream or sorbet will do the trick. But we all know these options don't hold a candle to anything homemade. Here we present some great easy recipes for frozen treats, chocolate goodies, fruit finales, and cookies. And to make things even easier we've taken some shortcuts (like using frozen puff pastry—the essential standby to pair with seasonal fruits) that skimp on time, not flavor. You'll also notice that some of our icy concoctions require special equipment, such as an ice-cream maker, ice-pop molds, or a manual ice-shaving machine, but they're well worth the investment.

Baked Alaska

SERVES 8
Active time: 20 min   Start to finish: 45 min

The key to this dessert is keeping the cake and the ice cream as cold as possible, so be sure not to thaw the cake or soften the ice cream before assembling. We recommend using ice cream in paper pints, so that they're easy to remove.

- 1 **(10¾-oz) frozen pound cake, not thawed**
- 2 **pt superpremium strawberry ice cream (not 1 qt)**
- 6 **large egg whites**
- ¼ **teaspoon fresh lemon juice**
- ¾ **cup sugar**

Cut frozen cake crosswise into ½-inch-thick slices. Line bottom of a 9-inch pie plate with some cake slices, halving or cutting into pieces to fill gaps. Halve a few more cake slices lengthwise and arrange around edge of plate, patching any gaps with pieces of remaining cake slices. (You may have a couple slices left over.)

Cut containers from ice cream and slice each pint into 3 rounds. Arrange 3 rounds in 1 layer on top of cake in pie plate and cut each remaining round into 6 wedges. Fill gaps in ice-cream layer with some wedges and mound remainder in center of pie plate. Freeze 25 minutes.

Preheat oven to 450°F.

After ice cream and cake have been freezing 20 minutes, beat egg whites with a pinch of salt using an electric mixer until foamy, then add lemon juice and continue to beat until whites just hold soft peaks. Gradually add sugar, beating, and continue to beat until whites just hold stiff, glossy peaks.

Remove ice-cream base from freezer and mound meringue over it, spreading to edge of plate to cover ice cream completely. Bake in middle of oven until meringue is golden brown, about 6 minutes. Serve immediately.

Cooks' notes:
- Cake and ice cream base can be assembled 2 days ahead and frozen, wrapped tightly. Make meringue and, after topping base, bake Alaska 10 minutes.
- The egg whites in this recipe are not fully cooked. If salmonella is a problem in your area, use powdered egg whites such as Just Whites.

clockwise from top left, strawberry margarita, mango daiquiri, blue martini, and camapri and grapefruit ice pops.

Note: All ice pops keep 1 week, frozen.

Strawberry Margarita Ice Pops

MAKES 8 (⅓-CUP) ICE POPS
Active time: 10 min   Start to finish: 24 hr

To make these grown-up ice pops nonalcoholic, substitute fresh orange juice for the tequila.

- 1¼ lb fresh strawberries, hulled and halved
- ½ cup white tequila
- ½ cup superfine granulated sugar
- 1 tablespoon fresh lime juice

Special equipment: 8 (⅓-cup) ice pop molds and 8 wooden sticks

Blend all ingredients in a blender until smooth, then force through a fine sieve into a large glass measuring cup. Pour into molds and add sticks. Freeze at least 24 hours.

Food editor Katy Massam, who made literally hundreds of ice pops while developing these recipes, found very little difference among the various plastic molds. The one from our local supermarket had plastic sticks attached to cheery red handles, and its volume was slightly less than that of the metal-topped molds, available, in season, at housewares shops. One tip if using the latter: When freezing a thin mixture—the Campari and grapefruit or even straight orange juice—let it firm up somewhat before inserting the sticks. Otherwise, the sticks slip sideways during freezing and the top of the mold won't come off. With a thicker mixture—the strawberry margarita, say—you can insert the sticks immediately. —JANE DANIELS LEAR

Mango Daiquiri Ice Pops

MAKES 8 (⅓-CUP) ICE POPS
Active time: 15 min   Start to finish: 24 hr

- 3 cups chopped peeled mangoes (2)
- 6 tablespoons light rum
- ½ cup superfine granulated sugar
- 1½ tablespoons fresh lime juice

Special equipment: 8 (⅓-cup) ice pop molds and 8 wooden sticks

Blend all ingredients with 2 tablespoons water in a blender until smooth, then force through a fine sieve into a large glass measuring cup. Pour into ice pop molds and add sticks. Freeze at least 24 hours.

Campari and Grapefruit Ice Pops

MAKES 9 (⅓-CUP) ICE POPS
Active time: 20 min   Start to finish: 24 hr

- ½ cup sugar
- 2 cups freshly squeezed pink grapefruit juice
- 3 tablespoons Campari
- 3 tablespoons vodka

Special equipment: 9 (⅓-cup) ice pop molds and 9 wooden sticks

Simmer sugar and ½ cup water in a small saucepan, stirring, until sugar is dissolved, then cool syrup. Stir in remaining ingredients, then pour through a fine sieve into a large glass measuring cup. Pour into molds and freeze at least 24 hours. Add sticks when mixture is slushy, about 1 hour.

ice pops

Blue Martini Ice Pops

MAKES 5 (⅓-CUP) ICE POPS
Active time: 25 min   Start to finish: 24 hr

Gins that emphasize fruit botanicals, such as Tanqueray No. Ten, work best in this recipe.

¼ cup sugar
6 strips fresh lemon zest
     (½ lemon)
3 tablespoons gin
2 tablespoons dry vermouth
1 tablespoon blue Curaçao

Special equipment: 5 (⅓-cup) ice pop
     molds and 5 wooden sticks

Simmer 1½ cups water, sugar, and zest in a small saucepan, stirring, until sugar is dissolved. Cool syrup, then stir in gin, dry vermouth, and Curaçao. Discard zest. Pour into molds and freeze at least 24 hours. Add sticks when mixture is slushy, about 1 hour.

Fresh Fruit Sno-Cones

MAKES ABOUT 10 (¾-CUP) SERVINGS
Active time: 15 min   Start to finish: 1¼ hr

1 lb fresh strawberries (about 1 qt),
     hulled and halved
6 oz fresh raspberries (about ½ pt)
½ cup sugar
7½ cups lightly packed shaved ice

Garnish: fresh berries
Special equipment: a manual
     ice-shaving machine

Coarsely mash strawberries, raspberries, and sugar in a bowl with a potato masher. Let berries stand, loosely covered, at room temperature, stirring occasionally, 1 hour.

Drain berry mixture in a fine sieve set over a bowl, pressing lightly on berries. Reserve crushed berries for another use.

For each serving, spoon 2½ tablespoons syrup over ¾ cup shaved ice. Serve immediately.

sno-cones

We understood how the sno-cone got its name after experimenting with a manual ice-shaving machine (available at Asian markets and from Pure Earth, 800-669-1376). Pop a bowl of ice into it, turn the crank, and, presto-change-o, you've got a pile of dry, fluffy snow—perfect for the fresh fruit sno-cones above. We tried an electric version but didn't like the wetter, denser, more crystallized result (or the heftier price tag). And hey, the manual machine is just too adorable for words—it's the ideal summertime countertop accoutrement. —JANE DANIELS LEAR

Mocha Rum Granita

MAKES ABOUT 1 QUART
Active time: 20 min   Start to finish: 2¼ hr

⅓ **cup sugar**
 1 **tablespoon dark rum**
 2 **tablespoons instant espresso powder**
1½ **oz fine-quality bittersweet chocolate
     (not unsweetened), chopped**

Bring sugar and 1½ cups water to a boil,
stirring until sugar is dissolved, then stir in rum.
Whisk together espresso powder and rum syrup
in a bowl until espresso powder is dissolved. Add
chocolate, whisking until chocolate is melted,
then cool.

Transfer mixture to a shallow metal baking
pan and freeze, stirring and crushing lumps with a
fork every 30 minutes, until firm but not frozen
hard, 2 to 3 hours. Before serving, scrape granita
with a fork to lighten texture.

Coconut Caramel Granita

MAKES ABOUT 1½ QUARTS
Active time: 20 min   Start to finish: 2¼ hr

⅔ **cup sugar**
 1 **(3½-oz) can sweetened flaked coconut
     (1 cup), coarsely chopped**

Cook sugar in a large deep skillet over
moderately high heat, stirring constantly with a
fork, until completely melted and a deep golden
caramel color. Carefully add 3 cups water
(mixture will bubble and steam) and cook,
stirring, until caramel is dissolved completely.
Stir together caramel and sweetened flaked
coconut in a bowl, then cool.

Transfer to a shallow metal baking pan and
freeze, stirring and crushing lumps with a fork
every 30 minutes, until firm but not frozen hard,
2 to 3 hours. Before serving, scrape granita with
a fork to lighten texture.

Sicilians love their granita, a sorbet-like treat made of frozen fruit-sweetened water. We took ours
to a whole new level, with mouthwatering flavors like mocha rum, coconut caramel, and
nectarine ginger. The beauty of this slushy ice treat is that it doesn't require
any fancy equipment at all. Simply stir together one of our favorite
stovetop concoctions, let it cool, pour it into a metal baking pan, and
freeze. True, you'll need to stir and crush ice lumps with a fork every
30 minutes for a few hours, but this minimal effort creates big flavor results. All of
our granitas can be made 3 days ahead of time. Re-scrape with a fork before serving.

granita

Nectarine Ginger Granita

MAKES ABOUT 1 QUART
Active time: 35 min   Start to finish: 2½ hr

**1 tablespoon peeled and coarsely chopped
    fresh ginger**
¼ cup sugar
**½ lb nectarines, pitted and chopped
    (1½ cups)**
1½ teaspoons fresh lemon juice

Finely chop ginger in a food processor or
blender. Add 1 cup water and blend well.
Transfer to a saucepan and stir in sugar. Bring
mixture to a boil, stirring until sugar is dissolved,
and simmer 5 minutes. Purée nectarines in food
processor and force through a fine sieve into a
bowl. Pour ginger mixture through sieve into
nectarines, pressing hard on solids, then whisk
in lemon juice and cool.

Transfer to a shallow metal baking pan and
freeze, stirring and crushing lumps with a fork
every 30 minutes, until firm but not frozen hard,
2 to 3 hours. Before serving, scrape granita with
a fork to lighten texture.

Persimmon Sorbet

MAKES ABOUT 1 QUART
Active time: 30 min   Start to finish: 3½ hr

*There are two main types of persimmons
available in the U. S.—Hachiya and Fuyu.
Hachiya (larger and acorn-shaped) can only be
consumed when very ripe. Fuyu (smaller and
tomato-shaped) are edible when soft or firm.*

⅔ cup sugar
**2 lb persimmons, cored, quartered,
    and seeded**
**1 tablespoon plus 1 teaspoon fresh
    lemon juice**

Special equipment: an ice-cream maker

Bring 1 cup water and sugar to a boil, stirring
until sugar is dissolved. Boil 3 minutes, then cool.
Scrape pulp from persimmons skins into a
blender and purée with lemon juice until very
smooth. Add sugar syrup and blend. Chill until
very cold, at least 2 hours.

Freeze mixture in ice-cream maker (or transfer
to a shallow metal baking pan and freeze, stirring
every 30 minutes, until slushy, about 2 hours.)
Transfer to an airtight container and freeze.
(Sorbet's consistency will remain soft.)

Cooks' note:
• Sorbet can be made 4 days ahead.

Vanilla-Bean Ice Cream

MAKES ABOUT 1½ QUARTS
Active time: 20 min   Start to finish: 4 hr

It's easy to think of vanilla as a backup singer instead of a superstar. But we wanted ours to shine, so we call for vanilla beans instead of extract and use whole eggs, not just yolks. The result is an ice cream that goes nicely with almost anything but is perfect on its own.

2 **cups heavy cream**
1 **cup whole milk**
¾ **cup sugar**
3 **vanilla beans, split lengthwise**
2 **large eggs**

Special equipment: an ice-cream maker

Stir together heavy cream, milk, sugar, and ⅛ teaspoon salt in a heavy saucepan. Scrape seeds from vanilla beans into cream mixture with tip of a knife, then drop in pods. Bring just to a boil.

Whisk eggs in a large bowl, then add hot cream mixture in a slow stream, whisking. Pour mixture into saucepan and cook over moderately low heat, stirring constantly with a wooden spoon, until slightly thickened and an instant-read thermometer registers 170°F (do not let boil). Pour custard through a fine sieve into a metal bowl, then cool, stirring occasionally. Chill, covered, until cold, at least 3 hours.

Freeze custard in ice-cream maker. Transfer to an airtight container and put in freezer to harden.

Cooks' notes:
• To cool custard quickly, set bowl in a larger bowl of ice and cold water and stir until chilled.
• Custard can chill up to 24 hours.

Ken Cameron, one of the world's leading experts on the vanilla orchid, tells cooks that, when it comes to vanilla beans, you really do get what you pay for. Each orchid is hand pollinated; the beans, or pods, take a long time to mature (the best are grown seven to eight inches before being cured); and the beans are hand harvested. As for vanilla extract, cooks should view the label "vanilla flavoring" with skepticism. The chemical vanillin which gives the flavoring its delicate spicy aroma and taste, is naturally produced by many plants and is a by product of the wood pulp industry. The hallmark of the real thing is "alcohol 35 percent," necessary for extracting vanillin from orchid pods. And the term *Bourbon vanilla* doesn't mean that you're getting a nip of Kentucky's finest; it refers to the origin of the beans—Under the Bourbon royals, French explorers transplanted orchids indigenous to Mexico and Central America, to colonies such as Tahiti and Madagascar. There are plantations in Mexico, but the orchid is virtually extinct in the wild. Madagascar beans are considered the finest, but the Mexican beans we ordered from Zingerman's (888-636-8162) were moist and very robust looking. We thought the flavor was about the same. —JANE DANIELS LEAR

Dried Cherry and Golden Raisin Turnovers

MAKES 4 TURNOVERS
Active time: 10 min   Start to finish: 35 min

1   **frozen puff pastry sheet
(from a 17¼-oz package), thawed**
3   **oz cream cheese, softened**
2   **tablespoons sugar**
¾   **cup mixed dried sour cherries and
golden raisins**
1   **large egg, lightly beaten**

Preheat oven to 400°F.

Quarter pastry sheet with a sharp knife to form 4 squares. Stir together cream cheese and 1½ tablespoons sugar, then divide among squares, spreading to leave a ¾-inch border all around. Sprinkle fruit over cream cheese, then brush some egg on pastry border. Fold each pastry into a triangle to enclose filling and crimp edges with a fork. Cut a small steam vent in top of each turnover. Brush tops with more egg and sprinkle with remaining ½ tablespoon sugar.

Bake on a lightly buttered baking sheet in lower third of oven until puffed and golden brown, about 25 minutes.

Figs with Vanilla Ice Cream and Aged Balsamic Vinegar

SERVES 4
Active time: 15 min   Start to finish: 15 min

12   **firm-ripe fresh figs, trimmed and
halved lengthwise**
3   **tablespoons turbinado sugar or light
brown sugar, forced through a sieve**
1   **pt superpremium vanilla ice cream**
1   **to 2 tablespoons aged balsamic vinegar**

Preheat broiler.

Arrange figs, cut sides up, in a large shallow baking pan. Sprinkle sugar evenly over fruit and broil 2 to 3 inches from heat until most of sugar is melted and deep golden in places, 3 to 5 minutes.

Immediately serve figs over ice cream, drizzled with vinegar.

Honeydew Melon in Coconut Milk

SERVES 8
Active time: 25 min   Start to finish: 35 min

1   **(14-oz) can well-stirred coconut milk**
3   **tablespoons sugar**
1½   **teaspoons fresh lime juice, or to taste**
1   **honeydew melon (5 lb), chilled**

Garnish: julienned lime zest
Special equipment: a melon-ball cutter

Stir together coconut milk, sugar, and lime juice in a small metal bowl until sugar is dissolved, then quick-chill in a metal bowl set in a larger bowl of ice and cold water, stirring occasionally, about 6 minutes.

Halve melon and discard seeds. Scoop melon into balls with cutter.

Divide melon among serving dishes, then pour coconut milk over top. Serve immediately.

Individual Tartes Tatin

MAKES 2 INDIVIDUAL TARTS
Active time: 10 min   Start to finish: 40 min

1   **frozen puff pastry sheet
        (from a 17¼-oz package), thawed**
2   **tablespoons unsalted butter**
¼   **cup packed light brown sugar**
1   **Golden Delicious apple, peeled,
        halved lengthwise, and cored**

Accompaniment: vanilla ice cream
Special equipment: 2 (1-cup) ramekins
        (3¼ inches across and 2¼ inches deep)

Preheat oven to 425°F.

Using a ramekin as a guide, cut 2 rounds from pastry sheet.

Heat butter in a 7-inch heavy skillet over moderate heat until foam subsides, then stir in brown sugar and 2 tablespoons water. Add apple halves and cook, turning frequently, 3 minutes. Put ramekins on a baking sheet and arrange an apple half, cored side up, in each. Top evenly with brown sugar sauce.

Cover apples with pastry rounds, letting edges of pastry hang over sides of apples. Bake tarts in middle of oven until pastry is puffed and deep golden brown, about 25 minutes, then cool on a rack 5 minutes. Working with 1 ramekin at a time, invert a plate over ramekin and invert ramekin onto plate. Carefully lift off ramekins.

Apricot Galette

SERVES 6
Active time: 20 min   Start to finish: 1 hr

¼   **cup sliced almonds**
¼   **cup confectioners sugar**
1   **frozen puff pastry sheet
        (from a 17¼-oz package), thawed**
6   **fresh apricots (preferably underripe
        and very tart), pitted and cut into
        ⅛-inch-thick wedges**
1   **tablespoon granulated sugar**

Accompaniment: lightly sweetened
        whipped cream

Preheat oven to 425°F.

Pulse almonds with confectioners sugar in a food processor until finely ground. Unfold pastry sheet on a lightly floured surface and cut out a 9-inch round. Transfer round to a buttered large shallow baking pan and prick pastry all over with a fork. Spoon almond mixture evenly over pastry, leaving a ¼-inch border. Arrange apricot wedges decoratively over almond mixture, overlapping them, and sprinkle with granulated sugar.

Bake *galette* in middle of oven until edges are golden brown, 30 to 35 minutes. Cool in pan on rack, 5 minutes, then transfer to serving plate.

Prosecco and Summer Fruit Terrine

SERVES 8
Active time: 15 min   Start to finish: 6¼ hr

Prosecco is a light and crisp Italian sparkling white wine with a hint of sweetness that pairs very well with fruit.

- **4 cups mixed fruit such as berries, peeled and thinly sliced peaches, and halved seedless grapes**
- **2¾ teaspoons unflavored gelatin (from two ¼-oz envelopes)**
- **2 cups Prosecco (Italian sparkling wine)**
- **½ cup sugar**
- **2 teaspoons fresh lemon juice**

Arrange fruit in a 1½-quart glass, ceramic, or nonstick terrine or loaf pan.

Sprinkle gelatin over ¼ cup Prosecco in a small bowl and let stand 1 minute to soften. Bring 1 cup Prosecco to a boil with sugar, stirring until sugar is dissolved. Remove from heat and add gelatin mixture, stirring until dissolved. Stir in remaining ¾ cup Prosecco and lemon juice, then transfer to a metal bowl set in a larger bowl of ice and cold water. Cool mixture, stirring occasionally, just to room temperature.

Slowly pour mixture over fruit, then chill, covered, until firm, at least 6 hours.

To unmold, dip pan in a larger pan of hot water 3 to 5 seconds to loosen. Invert a serving plate over terrine and invert terrine onto plate.

Cooks' note:
• Terrine can chill up to 3 days. Unmold just before serving.

Toffee McGreevey

MAKES ABOUT 2½ POUNDS
Active time: 25 min   Start to finish: 2¼ hr

Family recipes, fine-tuned from generation to generation, are often worth a try. This one, from Dawn McGreevey of Atlanta, is a favorite.

- **¾ lb slivered almonds (2¾ cups)**
- **2 sticks (1 cup) unsalted butter, cut into 16 pieces**
- **1 cup sugar**
- **6 tablespoons light corn syrup**
- **12 oz semisweet chocolate chips**

Special equipment: a candy thermometer

Preheat oven to 350°F and lightly oil a 15½- by 10½- by 1-inch metal baking pan.

Spread almonds in a shallow baking pan in 1 layer and toast in middle of oven until pale golden and fragrant, about 10 minutes. Cool nuts. Finely chop ½ cup almonds. Combine butter, sugar, corn syrup, a pinch of salt, and 2 tablespoons water in a 2- to 3-quart heavy saucepan and bring to a boil over moderately high heat, stirring until sugar is dissolved. Boil, stirring occasionally, until thermometer registers 290°F, about 7 minutes. Quickly stir in slivered almonds and immediately pour mixture into baking pan. Quickly spread toffee with an offset or wooden spatula in an even layer as close to edges of pan as possible.

Let toffee stand 1 minute (it will still be very hot), then sprinkle evenly with chocolate chips. When chips are melted, spread evenly over toffee with spatula. Sprinkle chopped almonds evenly over chocolate, gently pressing them to help adhere. Chill toffee until chocolate is firm, at least 2 hours (cover tightly with plastic wrap after 2 hours). Break into small pieces before serving.

Cooks' note:
• Toffee keeps 2 weeks, covered and chilled.

Chocolate Anise Bark

MAKES 6 PIECES
Active time: 15 min   Start to finish: 45 min

1 teaspoon anise seeds
⅓ cup dried sour cherries
⅓ cup dried apricots, coarsely chopped
⅓ cup salted roasted cashews,
   coarsely chopped
6 oz fine-quality bittersweet chocolate
   (not unsweetened), finely chopped

Special equipment: an electric
coffee/spice grinder

Line a small baking sheet with foil and chill.
Finely grind anise in coffee/spice grinder. Stir
together cherries, apricots, and cashews.

Melt chocolate in a double boiler or a small
metal bowl set over a small saucepan of barely
simmering water, stirring occasionally, until
smooth. Stir in anise and half of fruit, then spoon
onto center of baking sheet. Spread with a rubber
spatula into a roughly 10- by 5-inch rectangle and
sprinkle with remaining fruit mixture, pressing
lightly to help adhere. Chill until firm, about
30 minutes, then break into 6 pieces.

Cooks' note:
• Bark keeps 1 week, covered and chilled.

Chocolate Soufflé Cake with Orange Caramel Sauce

SERVES 8 TO 10
Active time: 1 hr   Start to finish: 2 hr

We love this cake for its lightness and intense chocolate flavor. The only difficult thing about it is remembering to take it easy when you fold the egg whites into the batter—the more gentle the folding, the airier the cake. And if you'd rather not make the orange caramel sauce, lightly sweetened whipped cream is a simple alternative.

- **2 sticks (1 cup) unsalted butter, cut into pieces**
- **9 oz fine-quality bittersweet chocolate (not unsweetened), chopped**
- **6 large eggs, separated**
- **⅔ cup plus ½ cup superfine granulated sugar**
- **3 navel or Valencia oranges**

Special equipment: a 10-inch springform pan

Make cake:

Put a small roasting pan filled halfway with hot water in bottom third of oven (to provide moisture during baking), then preheat oven to 325°F. Butter a 10-inch springform pan and line bottom with a round of parchment or wax paper, then butter paper.

Melt butter and chocolate together in a heavy saucepan over low heat, stirring, then remove from heat. Beat together yolks, ⅓ cup sugar, and ½ teaspoon salt in a large bowl with an electric mixer until thick and pale and ribbons form when beater is lifted, about 6 minutes. Beat whites at medium speed with cleaned beaters in another large bowl until they just hold soft peaks. Gradually add ⅓ cup sugar, beating until whites just hold stiff peaks. Stir warm chocolate into yolks until combined well. Stir one fourth of egg whites into chocolate mixture to lighten, then fold in remaining egg whites gently but thoroughly.

Pour batter into springform pan and bake in middle of oven (do not place springform pan in pan of hot water) until a tester inserted in center comes out with crumbs adhering, about 1 hour (a crust will form and crack on top of cake as it bakes). Transfer to a rack and cool 10 minutes (cake will "deflate" as it cools). Run a thin knife carefully around edge of cake, then remove side of pan. Cool cake on bottom of pan 30 minutes, then invert onto another rack or plate. Remove bottom of pan, then carefully peel off parchment. Invert cake onto a serving plate.

Make sauce while cake bakes:

Remove zest from 2 oranges in large strips and trim any white pith from zest. Cut zest into enough very thin strips to measure ¼ cup. Squeeze juice from 3 oranges and strain through a fine sieve. Measure out 1 cup juice.

Cook remaining ½ cup sugar in a dry heavy saucepan over moderate heat, undisturbed, until it begins to melt. Continue to cook, stirring occasionally with a fork, until sugar is melted and a deep golden caramel color. Add zest and cook, stirring, until fragrant, about 15 seconds. Tilt pan and carefully pour in juice (caramel will harden and steam vigorously). Cook over moderately low heat, stirring, until caramel is dissolved, then cool sauce.

Serve cake with orange sauce.

Cooks' note:
- We recommend making this cake 1 day ahead to allow flavors to develop. Keep chilled, covered with plastic wrap. Bring to room temperature before serving.

"Tea Cakes" (Sugar Cookies)

MAKES ABOUT 3½ DOZEN COOKIES
Active time: 20 min   Start to finish: 50 min

Sandra Crook of Jacksonville, Florida, serves these tea cakes warm, when they're nice and chewy, with jam or strawberries and cream. When cooled and left unadorned, they become crisp and buttery sugar cookies. She uses the Southerner's favorite flour, White Lily, which gives the tea cakes a wonderful crispness, but we also had good results when we tested the recipe with self-rising cake flour.

2½ **cups self-rising White Lily or
     cake flour**
 2 **sticks (1 cup) unsalted butter,
     softened**
1½ **cups sugar**
 1 **large egg, lightly beaten**
 1 **teaspoon vanilla**

Special equipment: a 2½- or 3-inch
     round cookie cutter

Preheat oven to 350°F.

Put flour in a bowl and make a well in center. Beat together butter and sugar in another bowl with an electric mixer until light and fluffy, then beat in egg and vanilla. Add butter mixture to well in flour, then incorporate it into flour with your fingertips just until dough comes together in a ball (do not overwork dough or it will be tough).

Halve dough and work with 1 half at a time. Roll out dough ¼-inch thick on a floured surface with a lightly floured rolling pin. Cut out cookies with floured cookie cutter (we used a fluted cutter), arranging cookies 1 inch apart on ungreased baking sheets. Reroll scraps once, using as little flour as possible, and cut out more cookies. Roll out and cut remaining dough in same manner.

Bake cookies in batches in middle of oven until very pale golden, 12 to 15 minutes. Cool on sheet 1 minute, then transfer to a rack to cool 5 minutes if serving warm, or to cool completely.

Cooks' notes:
• If your kitchen is very warm, chill dough to keep it from sticking to work surface.
• Cookies keep in an airtight container 1 week.

Star Anise Lace Cookies

MAKES ABOUT 48 COOKIES
Active time: 15 min   Start to finish: 1 hr

2   tablespoons star anise pieces
½   cup sugar
5   tablespoons unsalted butter
2   tablespoons balsamic vinegar
¼   cup all-purpose flour

Special equipment: an electric
   coffee/spice grinder and
   parchment paper

Preheat oven to 350°F.

Finely grind star anise in coffee/spice grinder. Bring anise, sugar, butter, and vinegar to a boil in a 1- to 1½-quart heavy nonstick saucepan over moderate heat, stirring, and boil 1 minute. Remove from heat and stir in flour and a pinch salt. Cool dough to room temperature, about 25 minutes.

Roll level ½-teaspoons dough into balls and arrange about 4 inches apart on 2 parchment-lined large baking sheets. Bake cookies in batches in upper and lower thirds of oven, switching position of sheets halfway through baking, until cookies are flat and golden, 7 to 10 minutes. Transfer cookies on parchment to racks to cool. Cool baking sheets and line with fresh parchment between batches.

Cooks' note:
• Cookies keep 5 days in an airtight container at
   room temperature.

Mom-Mom Fritch's Peanut Butter Cookies

MAKES ABOUT 70 COOKIES
Active time: 20 min   Start to finish: 50 min

We've been enjoying these cookies ever since Amy Fritch of New York City gave us the recipe a few years ago. One batch and you'll be hooked too.

1   cup peanut butter (creamy or chunky)
¾   cup sugar
1   large egg, lightly beaten
1   teaspoon baking soda

Preheat oven to 350°F.

Beat together peanut butter and sugar with a wooden spoon until combined well, then beat in egg and baking soda.

Roll level teaspoons of dough into balls and arrange about 1 inch apart on greased baking sheets. Flatten balls with tines of a fork to about 1½ inches in diameter, making a crosshatch pattern. Bake in batches in middle of oven until puffed and pale golden, about 10 minutes.

Cool cookies on baking sheets 2 minutes, then transfer with a metal spatula to racks to cool completely.

Cooks' note:
• Cookies keep 5 days in an airtight container at
   room temperature.

Menus

COOKING FOR family and friends is easy with these lunch and dinner ideas.

Spring/Summer Menus

MENU FOR 4

Slow-Roasted Tomatoes **21**

Chicken Breasts with Spinach, Prosciutto,
and Mozzarella **54**

Fried Potatoes **117**

Apricot Galette **151**

MENU FOR 4

Braised Lamb with Honey and Garlic **101**

Crisp Rosemary Potatoes **120**

Roasted Brussels Sprouts
with Garlic and Pancetta **125**

Chocolate Soufflé Cake
with Orange Caramel Sauce **154**

MENU FOR 4

Rhubarb Mint Coolers **33**

Sautéed Salmon with Gremolata **71**

Potato, Red Pepper, and Fennel Salad **123**

Nectarine Ginger Granita **147**

MENU FOR 4

Clams and Chorizo with Tomato and Garlic **71**

Corn Bread Supreme **118**

Fresh Fruit Sno-Cones **144**

MENU FOR 4 TO 6

Potato Chips **128**

Tarragon Lobster Salad **65**

Strawberry Margarita Ice Pops **143**

MENU FOR 4

Blue Cheese Hamburgers
with Caramelized Onions **94**

French-Fried Onion Rings **123**

Orzo, Radish, and Chive Salad
(double recipe) **124**

Mango Daiquiri Ice Pops **143**

VEGETARIAN MENU FOR 4

Two-Bean Salad **24**

Tomato, Goat Cheese, and Onion Tart **78**

Figs with Vanilla Ice Cream and
Aged Balsamic Vinegar **150**

VEGETARIAN MENU FOR 4

Cucumber and Cumin Soup (double recipe) **113**

Fennel, Leek, and Potato Gratin **80**

Prosecco and Summer Fruit Terrine **152**

MENU FOR 4

Fresh Mango and Cucumber Soup **113**

Grilled Pork Tenderloin with Mojo Sauce **97**

Zucchini Parmesan Fritters **119**

Mocha Rum Granita **146**

MENU FOR 6

Currant Mustard-Glazed Ham **100**

Green Beans with Lemon **125**

Fennel Mashed Potatoes **122**

Baked Alaska **141**

Fall/Winter Menus

MENU FOR 2

Red Bean and Ham Soup **110**

Corn Bread Supreme **118**

Individual Tartes Tatin **151**

MENU FOR 4

Daikon-Ginger Salad **25**

Stir-Fried Beef with Cilantro **93**

Coconut Caramel Granita **146**

MENU FOR 4

Mushroom Soup with Dill (double recipe) **108**

Weiner Schnitzel with Spaetzle **103**

Roasted Brussels Sprouts
with Garlic and Pancetta **125**

Individual Tartes Tatin (double recipe) **151**

VEGETARIAN MENU FOR 4

Carrot Ginger Soup **111**

Warm Lentil, Spinach, and Tomato Stew **85**

Chocolate Soufflé Cake
with Orange Caramel Sauce **154**

MENU FOR 4

Rib-Eye Steak au Poivre
with Balsamic Reduction **92**

Crisp Rosemary Potatoes **120**

Braised Leeks **124**

Vanilla-Bean Ice Cream **148**

MENU FOR 4

Turkey Burgers with Boursin **60**

Potato, Red Pepper, and Fennel Salad **123**

French-Fried Onion Rings **123**

Mom-Mom Fritch's Peanut Butter Cookies **157**

MENU FOR 4

Caldo Verde **107**

Poached Sole in White Wine Sauce **74**

Green Beans with Lemon (halve recipe) **125**

Mocha Rum Granita **146**

VEGETARIAN MENU FOR 4

Two-Bean Salad **24**

Baked Macaroni and Cheese
with Stewed Tomatoes **37**

Individual Tartes Tatin (double recipe) **151**

MENU FOR 4

Mustard Roasted Chicken **50**

Jerusalem Artichoke Purée
with Sage and Parmesan **117**

Dried Cherry and Golden Raisin Turnovers **150**

MENU FOR 6

Corn and Garlic Soup **110**

Cider-Braised Pork Shoulder
with Caramelized Onions **99**

Fennel Mashed Potatoes **122**

Chocolate Soufflé Cake
with Orange Caramel Sauce **154**

Index

Page numbers in italics indicate color photographs
 indicates recipes that can be prepared
in 30 minutes or less
indicates recipes that are one-dish meals

A

G

M

Acknowledgments

COMING UP WITH DELICIOUS, well-rounded, dishes using only five ingredients is definitely a challenge—one that *Gourmet*'s food editors face each month for the Five Ingredients column. So when asked to create over 100 new dishes for this cookbook, they were ready for the task. Day after day, so many flavorful treats appeared that the most common cry heard in the test kitchen was, "This is only *five* ingredients!?" We would like to thank Alexis Touchet, Lori Powell (who also styled the front of jacket recipe), Shelley Wiseman, Ruth Cousineau, Gina Miraglia (who created the front of jacket tart), Melissa Roberts, and Ian Knauer. Special thanks to Zanne Stewart, Executive Food Editor, and Kempy Minifie, Senior Food Editor, for lending us their expertise and tastebuds, and to Jane Daniels Lear for her informative text.

We'd like to thank Romulo Yanes, *Gourmet*'s photographer (who doubled as prop stylist), and his assistant Stephanie Foley, for page after page of glorious color. Deborah Ory shot the iconic chapter openers (the wishbone and old-fashioned eggbeater appear courtesy of *Gourmet* Editor James Rodewald). Additional photographs were contributed by Alan Richardson, Craig Cutler, Maura McEvoy, and Rita Maas.

Anne Wright, with the aid of Maureen O'Connor, carefully pieced the manuscript together at Bill Smith Studios, while Richard Elman of Random House shepherded the book through color corrections and printing. *Gourmet* Editor Cheryl Brown was our top editor and extra pair of eyes, and John Haney, *Gourmet* copy chief, handled our many queries.

Finally, we'd like to give special thanks to Audrey Razgaitis and *Gourmet* Art Director Diana LaGuardia for designing pages as fresh and colorful as the recipes themselves.

The Editors of Gourmet Books

Table Setting Acknowledgments

Any items not credited are privately owned.

Cool Drinks
Rhubarb Mint Coolers
Page 33: "Fifties" highball glasses—Ad Hoc Softwares, (212-925-2652).

Pasta
Linguine with Scallion Sauce and Sautéed Shrimp
Page 40: Ceramic dinner plate by Aletha Soule—for stores call The Loom Company, (212-366-7214).

Fish & Shellfish
Tarragon Lobster Salad
Page 64: Jadite bowl—ABC Carpet & Home (212-473-3000).

Vegetarian Main Dishes
Fried Eggs and Asparagus with Parmesan
Page 82: Ceramic oven-to-table gratin dish by Chantal—Bloomingdale's (800-555-7467).

Meats
Rib-Eye Steak au Poivre with Balsamic Reduction
Page 92: "Tric" porcelain plates and bowls by Arzberg—for store information, (800-296-7508).

Side Dishes
Fennel Mashed Potatoes
Page 122: Ceramic bowl from Pottery Barn, (212-753-5424).

Snacks
Potato Chips
Page 128: Vintage European hotel silver-plate bowl from Hôtel—Bergdorf Goodman, 754 Fifth Avenue, New York City.

Sweets
Fresh Fruit Sno-Cones
Page 145: Glass—moss (212-226-2190).
Vanilla-Bean Ice Cream
Page 149: Platter and ceramic tea bowls—ABC Carpet & Home.

Photo Credits

We gratefully acknowledge the photographers listed below.
With a few exceptions, their work was previously published in *Gourmet* magazine.

Craig Cutler: Strawberry Margarita Ice Pops, Mango Daiquiri Ice Pops, Campari and Grapefruit Ice Pops, and Blue Martini Ice Pops (p. 142). Copyright © 2000.

Rita Maas: Peach Sangría, back jacket (p. 6, p. 28). Copyright © 2000. Coffee Avocado Milkshakes (p. 31). Copyright © 2001. Fresh Fruit Sno-Cones (p. 145). Copyright © 2001.

Maura McEvoy: Green Beans with Lemon (p. 7, p. 125). Copyright © 2000. Rutabaga and Carrot Purée (p. 117). Copyright © 2000.

Deborah Ory: Plate and fork (p. 13). Glass with ice (p. 27). Pasta (p. 35). Wishbone (p. 49). Fork (p. 63). Radish (p. 77). Cleaver (p. 91). Spoon (p. 105). Casserole dish (p. 115). Napkin (p. 127). Egg beater (p. 139). All photographs copyright © 2002.

Alan Richardson: Mussels with Potatoes and Spinach (p. 7, p. 69). Copyright © 2000. Slow-Roasted Tomatoes (p. 21). Copyright © 1999. Oven-Poached Fish in Olive Oil (p.75). Copyright © 2000. Carrot and Radish Salad (p. 116). Copyright © 2000. Persimmon Sorbet (p. 147). Copyright © 2000.

Romulo Yanes: Tomato, Goat Cheese, and Onion Tart, front jacket (p. 8, p. 79). Copyright © 2002. Salt and Pepper Shrimp, back jacket (p. 14). Copyright © 2001. Vanilla-Bean Ice Cream, back jacket (p. 149). Copyright © 2000. Baked Macaroni and Cheese with Stewed Tomatoes, back jacket, (p. 36). Copyright © 2002. Cider-Braised Pork Shoulder with Caramelized Onions, back jacket (p. 98). Copyright © 2001. Pasta with Asparagus-Lemon Sauce, back jacket, (p. 47). Copyright © 2000. Turkey Burger with Boursin, back jacket (p. 2, p. 61). Copyright © 2002. Fresh Mango and Cucumber Soup, back jacket (p. 112). Copyright © 2002. Bunch of herbs (p. 1, p. 11). Copyright © 2002. Chile peppers (p. 5, p. 10). Copyright © 2002. Speedy Pizzas (p. 6, p. 131). Copyright © 2001. Olive-Stuffed Chicken with Almonds (p. 6, p. 51). Copyright © 2001. Lemons (p. 6, p. 10). Copyright © 2002. Linguine with Scallion Sauce and Sautéed Shrimp (p. 6, p. 40). Copyright © 1999. Rib-Eye Steak au Poivre with Balsamic Reduction (p. 6, p. 92). Copyright © 2000. Fried Eggs and Asparagus with Parmesan (p. 7, p. 82). Copyright © 2001. Roasted Tomato Soup with Goat Cheese Croûtes (p. 7, p. 109). Copyright © 2002. Baked Alaska (p. 7, p. 140). Copyright ©

2001. Tuna Empanaditas (p. 7, p. 17). Copyright © 2001. Garlic (p. 7, p. 11). Copyright © 2002. Butter (p. 6). Copyright © 2002. Salt (p. 6). Copyright © 2002. Honeycomb (p. 7). Copyright © 2002. Cured meats (p. 7). Copyright © 2002. Potato Latkes (p. 22). Copyright © 2000. Rhubarb Mint Coolers (p. 33). Copyright © 1999. Braised Chicken with Shallots, Garlic, and Balsamic Vinegar (p. 56). Copyright © 2001. Copyright © 2002. Tarragon Lobster Salad (p. 64). Copyright © 2001. Romaine-Wrapped Halibut (p. 70). Copyright © 2001. Ricotta Gnocchi with Roasted Tomato (p. 86). Copyright © 2000. Oven-Braised Beef with Tomato Sauce and Garlic (p. 94). Copyright © 2001. Braised Short Ribs with Dijon Mustard (p. 96). Copyright © 2000. Lamb Chops with Coarse-Grain Mustard, (p. 101). Copyright © 2001. Corn Bread Supreme (p. 118). Copyright © 2000. Glazed Turnips (p. 121). Copyright © 2001. Fennel Mashed Potatoes (p. 122). Copyright © 1998. Potato Chips (p. 128). Copyright © 1997. Cream Drop Biscuits (p. 134). Copyright © 2001. Meyer Lemon Marmalade (p. 136). Copyright © 1999. Apricot Gallette (p. 151). Copyright © 1999. Chocolate Anise Bark (p. 153).

Copyright © 2000. Chocolate Soufflé Cake with Orange Caramel Sauce (p. 155). Copyright © 2001. "Tea Cakes" (Sugar Cookies) (p. 156). Copyright © 2000.